A Thimbleberries®
Housewarming

LYNETTE JENSEN

RODALE

© 2000 Lynette Jensen

Thimbleberries Contributing Editors: Sue Bahr, Darlene Zimmerman

Developmental Editor: Barbara Konzak Kuhn

Technical Editor: Beate Nellemann

Production Director: Diane Pedersen

Thimbleberries Contributing Illustrator: Lisa Kirchoff

Cover Design: Christina Jarumay

Book Design: Kristen Yenche

Illustrator: Tammy Tribble and Claudia Böhm © C&T Publishing

Photographer: Keith Evenson, Photo on page 6: Sharon Risedorph

Front Cover Image: *Lost Mittens*

Back Cover Images: *Cherry Basket* and *Tulips, Tulips*

Attention teachers: C&T Publishing, Inc. encourages you to use this book as a text for teaching. Contact them at 800-284-1114 or www.ctpub.com for more information about the C&T Teacher's Program. Questions concerning projects and instructions should be directed to C&T Publishing, 1-800-284-1114.

Printed in the United States of America

Rodale Inc. makes every effort to use acid free ∞, recycled paper ♻.

ISBN 1–57954–612–9

10 9 8 7 6 5 4 3 2 1 hardcover

C&T Publishing edition published 2000

Rodale Inc. edition June 2002

WE **INSPIRE** AND **ENABLE** PEOPLE TO IMPROVE
THEIR LIVES AND THE WORLD AROUND THEM

Table of Contents

Homemaking is my passion...

As long as I can remember, I have been accessorizing my surroundings. I love the idea of "home" and all that it entails.

My early recollections of "housewarming" center around my first playhouse, built from bricks stacked near my mother's garden. Her beautiful garden provided me with lots of fresh produce and many ingredients for all the special recipes a young child concocts. I made my healthy share of mud pies in the playhouse, using a heart-shaped iron pancake griddle. I was also surrounded by a seemingly endless supply of fresh flowers, which I used generously in my little house—just as my mother gathered her bouquets for our tables indoors.

As early as spring weather would allow, "playing house" outside would resume. I remember the details as vividly as if it were yesterday...including the day my heart was broken when I learned the bricks were sold to a neighbor. Yet, my parents had a wonderful surprise for me. My little roofless one-room brick playhouse was soon replaced with a chicken coop from my grandmother's farm. One whole wall, from floor to ceiling, was made from a bank of paned windows. My new house was glorious! I decorated and redecorated the house over and over for years to come—changing the feed sack curtains, making tablecloths, designing doll blankets—making my little house my home. To this day, filling a home with collectibles and handmade items defines my personal style.

In my early years of marriage the apartments and homes my husband and I lived in were temporary and very modest. I became intrigued and challenged by the task of personalizing my surroundings on a very limited budget. Then, as now, creativity is the answer. The most creative—and economical answer—is new paint, second-hand furniture, and, of course, fabric. A room can be totally transformed with throw pillows, a simple curtain or valance, and a quilt. The construction of the additions need not be complicated: good color and simple design are often the successful solution.

I love referring to my home as my "nest" and I look to have every room reflect my interests and passions. Therefore, I use quilts generously throughout the house. Quilts are the mainstay of my decorating style. They help turn my house into a warm, inviting home. Having a quilt for every room in the house is an ultimate dream. The pages of this book are filled with a wide variety of quilt designs, big and small, to enhance and personalize your home.

Whether you are in your first home, redecorating, or perhaps helping a loved one with home projects, *A Thimbleberries Housewarming* is sure to make the task enjoyable. My goal is to create projects that are not only good-looking but also attainable. Because we have all become very busy with jobs, families, and a variety of volunteer commitments and leisure activities, our time is limited. It is important to have quilt projects that go together quickly and successfully so the craft remains a joy and not a chore. With our modern lifestyle, as fast-paced as our lives have become and as more technology is introduced, there seems to be a need to soften our surroundings and stay connected to the past and to family. Helping others achieve this goal through quiltmaking is personally very rewarding.

Quiltmaking is a very special and personal way to create a warm, inviting home for your family. My hope is that the collection of projects that follow will warm your house and your heart.

My Best,

Lynette Jensen

Make Yourself at *Home*...

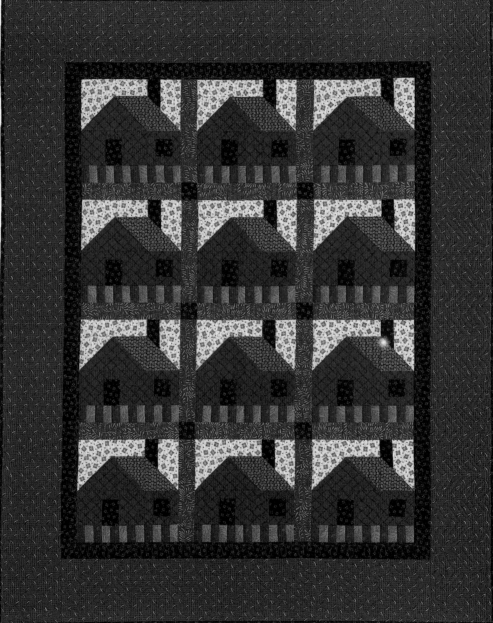

A quilt says "welcome" to all who enter a room. A quilt immediately softens a room and sets an inviting tone. Since quiltmaking is a true heritage craft, it brings a sense of the past into our present-day surroundings. A handmade quilt is a very unique, one-of-a-kind accessory that sets a room apart from the ordinary. Quilts impart a message..."come in, sit down, make yourself at home."

Summer Stars

58 x 72-inches

FABRICS AND SUPPLIES

Yardage is based on 42-inch wide fabric.

- 1½ yards Green Print for blocks and middle border

- 1⅛ yards Rose Print for stars

- 1 yard Beige Print for background

- 2¼ yards Beige Floral for lattice, inner and outer borders

- ⅔ yard Binding fabric

- 3½ yards Backing fabric

- Quilt batting, at least 62 x 76-inches

- Rotary cutter, mat, and wide clear-plastic ruler with ⅛-inch markings are necessary tools in attaining accuracy. A 6 x 24-inch ruler is recommended.

STAR BLOCKS
Make 12

Green Print fabric:
Cut three 2½ x 42-inch strips. Cut the strips into forty eight 2½-inch squares.

Cut six 2½ x 42-inch strips. Cut the strips into forty eight 2½ x 4 ½-inch rectangles.

Cut two 4½ x 42-inch strips. Cut the strips into twelve 4½-inch squares.

Rose Print fabric:
Cut two 2⅞ x 42-inch strips. Cut the strips into twenty four 2⅞-inch squares.

Cut three 2½ x 42-inch strips. Cut the strips into forty eight 2½-inch squares.

Cut eight 2½ x 42-inch strips. Cut the strips into forty eight 2½ x 6 ½-inch rectangles.

This light, airy quilt is reminiscent of warm summer days and nights.

A good piece of porch or patio furniture can serve as a side piece indoors as well. Bring a bit of summer into your home year round with this patchwork of summer colors.

FABRIC KEY

Green Print

Rose Print

Beige Print

Beige Floral

Beige Print fabric:

Cut two $2^7/8$ x 42-inch strips. Cut the strips into twenty four $2^7/8$-inch squares.

Cut six $2^1/2$ x 42-inch strips. Cut the strips into ninety six $2^1/2$-inch squares.

Cut three $2^1/2$ x 42-inch strips. Cut the strips into twenty four, $2^1/2$ x $4^1/2$-inch rectangles.

PIECING

Step 1

Layer the $2^7/8$-inch Rose and Beige squares right sides together in pairs. Cut the layered squares in half diagonally. Stitch $1/4$-inch from the diagonal edge of each pair of triangles, and press.

MAKE 48
$2^1/2$-INCH TRIANGLE-PIECED SQUARES

Step 2

Position the $2^1/2$-inch Beige squares at the corners of the $2^1/2$ x $6^1/2$-inch Rose rectangles. Draw a diagonal line on the Beige squares and stitch on the line. Trim the seam allowances to $1/4$-inch, and press.

MAKE 48

Step 3

Position $2^1/2$-inch Rose squares at the corner of $2^1/2$ x $4^1/2$-inch Beige rectangles. Draw a diagonal line on the Rose squares and stitch on the line. Trim the seam allowances to $1/4$-inch, and press. Position the remaining $2^1/2$-inch Rose squares at the opposite corner of the Beige rectangles. Draw a diagonal line on the Rose squares, then stitch, trim, and press.

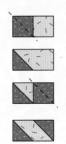

MAKE 24

Step 4

Sew together two $2^1/2$-inch Green squares, one $2^1/2$ x $4^1/2$-inch Green rectangle, and two triangle-pieced squares, then press.

MAKE 24

Step 5

Sew together two units from Step 2, and press.

MAKE 24

Step 6

Sew together two $2^1/2$ x $4^1/2$-inch Green rectangles, one $4^1/2$-inch Green square, and two units from Step 3, and then press.

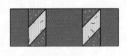

MAKE 12

Step 7

Sew together two units from Step 4, two units from Step 5, and one unit from Step 6. At this point each block should measure $12^1/2$-inches square.

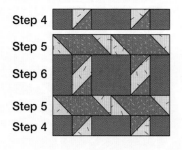

Step 4
Step 5
Step 6
Step 5
Step 4

MAKE 12

LATTICE AND BORDERS

Note: The yardage given allows for the lattice and border strips to be cut on the crosswise grain. Diagonally piece the strips as needed.

Beige Floral fabric:

Cut three 2½ x 42-inch strips. From these strips cut eight 2½ x 12½-inch lattice strips.

Cut five 2½ x 42-inch strips. From these strips cut five 2½ x 40½-inch horizontal lattice/inner border strips.

Cut three 2½ x 42-inch strips. From these strips cut two 2½ x 58½-inch long lattice/inner border strips.

Cut seven 6½ x 42-inch strips for the outer border.

Green Print fabric:

Cut six 1½ x 42-inch strips for the middle border.

PIECING

Step 1

Join three Star blocks with two 2½ x 12½-inch Beige Floral lattice strips, and press. Make 4 rows.

Step 2

Join the rows of blocks with horizontal 2½ x 40½-inch Beige Floral lattice strips, and press. Sew Beige Floral lattice/inner border strips to the top and bottom of the quilt, and press.

Step 3

Sew the 2½ x 58½-inch Beige Floral lattice/inner border strips to the sides of the quilt, and press.

ATTACHING THE BORDERS

Step 1

Measure the quilt from left to right through the center. Cut two 1½-inch wide Green middle border strips to this measurement. Sew to the top and bottom of the quilt, and press.

Step 2

Measure the quilt from top to bottom through the center. Cut two 1½-inch wide Green middle border strips to this measurement. Sew to the sides of the quilt, and press.

Step 3

Measure the quilt from left to right through the center. Cut two 6½-inch wide Beige Floral outer borders to this measurement. Sew to the top and bottom of the quilt, and press.

Step 4

Measure the quilt from top to bottom through the center. Cut two 6½-inch wide Beige Floral outer borders to this measurement. Sew to the sides of the quilt, and press.

PUTTING IT ALL TOGETHER

Step 1

Trim the backing and batting so they are 4-inches larger than the quilt top dimensions.

Step 2

Mark quilting designs on the quilt top. Layer the backing, batting and quilt top, and quilt as desired. When the quilting is complete, hand baste a scant 1/4-inch from the quilt top edge. Trim excess batting, and backing even with the quilt top.

BINDING

From the binding fabric:

Cut seven $2^3/4$ x 42-inch strips.

Sew the binding to the quilt using a $3/8$-inch seam allowance. This measurement will produce a 1/2-inch finished double binding.

BINDING AND DIAGONAL PIECING

See General Instructions page 140.

A Welcoming Touch...

Colors and motifs in a quilt can unite the outdoors with the style and furnishings of the interior of the home.

An antique laundry basket filled with light summer quilts is a nice addition to the porch for those evenings when there may be a little chill in the air.

Folk Art

Flowers

22-inches square

FABRICS AND SUPPLIES

Yardage is based on 42-inch wide fabric.

- $1/2$ yard Blue Print for center block and outer border

- $4^{1}/_{2}$-inch square Brown Plaid for quilt center

- $1/2$ yard Tan Plaid for background

- $1/8$ yard Green Print for leaf appliqués

- $1/8$ yard Red Print for flower appliqués

- $4^{1}/_{2}$-inch square Gold Print for flower centers

- $1/3$ yard Binding fabric

- $3/4$ yard Backing fabric

- $1/2$ yard paper-backed fusible webbing

- Quilt batting, at least 26-inches square

- #8 Black pearl cotton, or one skein of embroidery floss

- Rotary cutter, mat, and wide clear-plastic ruler with $1/8$-inch markings are necessary tools for attaining accuracy. A 6 x 24-inch ruler is recommended.

CENTER BLOCK

Blue Print fabric:
Cut one $2^{1}/_{2}$ x 42-inch strip. From this strip cut two $2^{1}/_{2}$ x $4^{1}/_{2}$-inch strips and two $2^{1}/_{2}$ x $8^{1}/_{2}$-inch strips.

Cut one $2^{7}/_{8}$ x 42-inch strip.

Brown Plaid fabric:
Cut one $4^{1}/_{2}$-inch square.

Tan Plaid fabric:
Cut one $2^{7}/_{8}$ x 42-inch strip.

Cut four $2^{1}/_{2}$-inch squares.

U*se colorful napkins as a decorating accessory. Fold the napkin as you would a paper fan. Fold it in half and let the color and pattern unfold.*

C*ollect interesting naturals such as pinecones, pods, and acorns, to add a little texture and color to antique bowls.*

Fabric Key

Tan Plaid

Blue Print

Brown Plaid

Red Print

Green Print

Gold Print

PIECING

Step 1

Sew a 2½ x 4½-inch Blue Print rectangle to the top and bottom of the 4½-inch Brown Plaid square, and press.

Step 2

Sew 2½ x 8½-inch Blue Print strips to the sides of the Step 1 unit, and press.

Step 3

To make the sawtooth sections, layer the 2⅞ x 42-inch Blue Print and Tan Plaid strips together, and press. Cut the layered strips into 2⅞-inch squares, taking care not to shift the layers as you cut.

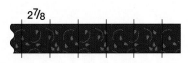

CROSSCUT 8

Step 4

Cut the layered squares in half diagonally. Stitch ¼-inch from the diagonal edge of each pair of triangles, and press. At this point each triangle-pieced square should measure 2½-inches square.

MAKE 16

Step 5

Sew four triangle-pieced squares together, and press.

MAKE 4 SETS

Step 6

Sew two Step 5 sections to the top and bottom of the Step 2 square, and press.

Step 7

Sew a 2½-inch Tan Plaid square to the ends of the remaining two sections, and press. Sew to the sides of the block, and press.

BORDERS

Note: The yardage given allows for the border strips to be cut on the crosswise grain.

Tan Plaid fabric:

Cut two 3 x 42-inch strips for inner borders.

Blue Print fabric:

Cut three 3 x 42-inch strips for outer borders.

ATTACHING THE BORDERS

Step 1

Measure the block from left to right through the center. Cut two 3-inch-wide Tan Plaid border strips to this measurement. Sew the border strips to the top and bottom of the block, and press.

Step 2

Measure the block from top to bottom through the center. Cut two 3-inch-wide Tan Plaid border strips to this measurement. Sew the border strips to the sides of the block, and press.

Step 3

Measure the quilt as you did in Step 1. Cut two 3-inch wide Blue Print border strips to this measurement. Sew the border strips to the top and bottom of the quilt, and press.

Step 4

Measure the quilt as you did in Step 2. Cut two 3-inch wide Blue Print border strips to this measurement. Sew the border strips to the sides of the quilt, and press.

FUSIBLE WEB APPLIQUÉ

Step 1

The appliqué shapes are on page 19. The decorative stitches can be found on page 101. Trace the shapes the required number of times, leaving $1/2$-inch between each shape. Cut out each shape roughly $1/4$-inch outside the traced lines.

Step 2

Press the fusible webbing shapes to the back of the fabrics chosen for each appliqué. Let cool, then cut out the shapes on the drawn line. Peel off the paper from the fabric.

Step 3

Position the appliqué shapes on the quilt corners, overlapping where needed. See the quilt diagram for placement. Fuse in place following manufacturer's directions.

Step 4

Using the buttonhole stitch (see page 101) and three strands of floss or one of black pearl cotton thread, stitch around the flowers, centers, and leaves.

PUTTING IT ALL TOGETHER

Step 1

Trim the batting and backing so they are 4-inches larger than the quilt top.

Step 2

Mark quilting designs on the quilt top. Layer the batting, backing, and quilt top, and quilt as desired. When the quilting is complete, hand baste a scant $1/4$-inch from the edge of the quilt top. Trim off excess batting and backing.

BINDING

From the binding fabric:
Cut three $2 1/4$ x 42-inch strips.

Sew the binding to the quilt with a $1/4$-inch seam allowance. This measurement will produce a $3/8$-inch wide finished double binding.

BINDING AND DIAGONAL PIECING

See General Instructions on page 140.

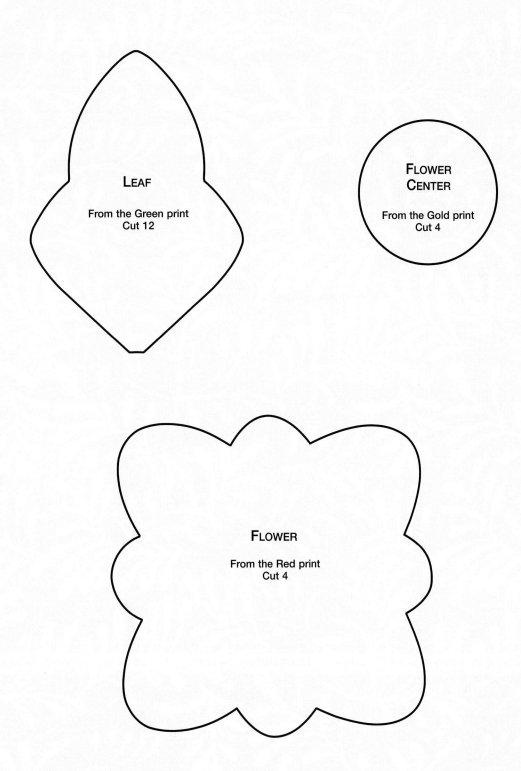

LEAF

From the Green print
Cut 12

FLOWER
CENTER

From the Gold print
Cut 4

FLOWER

From the Red print
Cut 4

Apple a *Day*

14 x 18-inches

FABRICS AND SUPPLIES

Yardage is based on 42-inch wide fabric.

- Fat quarter Red Print for apple and outer border

- Fat quarter Beige Print for background, middle border, and pieced border

- $\frac{1}{2}$ yard Green Print for leaves, inner border, pieced border, and binding

- Fat quarter Brown Print for apple stem and corner squares

- $\frac{1}{2}$ yard Backing fabric

- Quilt batting, at least 18 x 22-inches

- Rotary cutter, mat, and wide clear-plastic ruler with $\frac{1}{8}$-inch markings are necessary tools in attaining accuracy. A 6 x 24-inch ruler is recommended.

APPLE BLOCK

Red Print fabric:
Cut one $4\frac{1}{2}$-inch square.

Beige Print fabric:
Cut one $2\frac{1}{4}$ x $5\frac{1}{2}$-inch rectangle.
Cut one $2\frac{1}{4}$ x $4\frac{1}{2}$-inch rectangle.

Cut two $1\frac{1}{2}$ x $10\frac{1}{2}$-inch strips.

Cut one $1\frac{1}{2}$ x $4\frac{1}{2}$-inch rectangle.

Cut one $1\frac{1}{2}$ x $2\frac{1}{4}$-inch rectangle.

Cut four $1\frac{1}{2}$-inch squares.

Cut one 1 x 2-inch rectangle.

Green Print fabric:
Cut two $2\frac{1}{4}$-inch squares.

Brown Print fabric:
Cut one 1 x $4\frac{1}{2}$-inch rectangle.

Look for shutters, old doors and architectural panels. Mount the quilt on wood instead of framing it. This adds a great deal of interest to a plain wall and is so inexpensive.

Store scented votives in the open to take advantage of their scent and decorative color.

Get big decorating value for very little money by using interesting twigs and branches—here, red twig dogwood and birch—to make a simple arrangement.

FABRIC KEY

Red Print

Beige Print

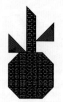

Green Print

Brown Print

PIECING

Step 1

Position 1½-inch Beige squares on the corners of the 4½-inch Red square. Draw diagonal lines on the squares and stitch on the lines. Trim the seam allowances to ¼-inch, and press.

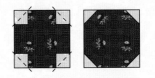

Step 2

Position a 2¼-inch Green square on the corner of the 2¼ x 5½-inch Beige rectangle and on the corner of the 2¼ x 4½-inch Beige rectangle. Referring to the diagrams, draw diagonal lines on the squares and stitch on the lines. Trim the seam allowances to ¼-inch, and press. Add the 1½ x 2¼-inch Beige rectangle to Leaf B.

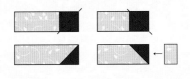

LEAF A   LEAF B

Step 3

Position the 1 x 2-inch Beige rectangle on the corner of the 1 x 4½-inch Brown rectangle. Referring to the diagram, draw a diagonal line on the Beige rectangle and stitch on the line. Trim the seam allowance to ¼-inch, and press.

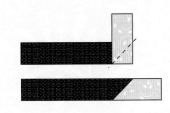

Step 4

Referring to the quilt diagram, sew the leaf units to both sides of the stem unit, and press. Sew this unit to the top of the apple unit, and press. Sew the 1½ x 4½-inch Beige rectangle to the bottom of the block, and sew the 1½ x 10½-inch Beige rectangles to the sides of the block, and press. At this point the block should measure 6½ x 10½-inches.

BORDERS

Note: The yardage given allows for the border strips to be cut on the crosswise grain.

Green Print fabric:

Cut two 1 x 6½-inch strips for the top and bottom inner borders.

Cut two 1 x 11½-inch strips for the side inner borders.

Cut one 2½ x 42-inch strip. From this strip cut twenty 1½ x 2½-inch rectangles for the pieced borders.

Beige Print fabric:

Cut two 1 x 7½-inch strips for the top and bottom middle borders.

Cut two 1 x 12½-inch strips for the side middle borders.

Cut three 1½ x 21-inch strips. From these strips cut forty 1½-inch squares for the pieced borders.

Red Print fabric:

Cut two 2½ x 10½-inch strips for the top and bottom outer borders.

Cut two 2½ x 18½-inch strips for the side outer borders

Brown Print fabric:

Cut four 1½-inch corner squares.

ATTACHING THE BORDERS

Step 1

Attach the 1-inch wide Green inner border, and press.

Step 2

Attach the 1-inch wide Beige middle border, and press.

Step 3

Position 1½-inch Beige squares on the corner of each 1½ x 2½-inch Green rectangle. Draw a diagonal line on the squares and stitch on the line. Trim the seam allowances to ¼-inch, and press. Repeat this process for the opposite corner of the rectangle.

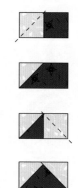

MAKE 20

Step 4

Sew four triangle units together for the top and bottom borders. Sew the borders to the quilt, and press.

Step 5

Sew six triangle units together for the side borders. Add 1½-inch Brown squares to both ends of the borders. Sew the borders to the quilt, and press. At this point the quilt should measure 10½ x 14½-inches.

Step 6

Attach the 2½-inch wide Red outer border, and press.

PUTTING IT ALL TOGETHER

Trim the backing and batting so they are 4-inches larger than the quilt top dimensions. Mark quilting designs on the quilt top. Layer the backing, batting, and quilt top, and quilt as desired. When quilting is complete, hand baste the three layers together a scant ¼-inch from the quilt top edge. Trim excess batting and backing even with the quilt top.

BINDING

Green Print fabric:

Cut two 2¼ x 42-inch strips.

Sew the binding to the quilt using a ¼-inch seam allowance. This measurement will produce a ⅜-inch wide finished double binding.

BINDING AND DIAGONAL PIECING

See General Instructions on page 140.

A Welcoming Touch...

A small quilt becomes artwork rather than only a piece of craftwork when it is framed. It makes a strong visual statement and also announces to all who enter that color, design, and needlework is valued in the home. More importantly, it is a piece of original artwork!

If the entrance has vaulted ceilings or plain walls with no room for furniture, a large quilt would add a dynamic splash of color and design to an otherwise difficult spot to decorate. The bold color and design draws those who enter into your home and sets the mood for what is to follow.

Pumpkins for *Sale*

40-inches square

FABRICS AND SUPPLIES

Yardage is based on 42-inch wide fabric.

- $1/8$ yard Green Print #1 for a leaf block and pumpkin stems

- $1/8$ yard each of six assorted Prints, Plaids, or Florals in Green, Brown, and Orange for leaf blocks

- $5/8$ yard Beige Print for background

- $8^1/2$ x $10^1/2$-inch piece of Orange Print #1 for small pumpkin

- $1/4$ yard Orange Print #2 for large pumpkin

- $1/3$ yard Brown Print for inner border

- $1/4$ yard Black Print for sawtooth border

- $3/4$ yard Russet Print for outer border

- $1/2$ yard Binding fabric

- $1^1/4$ yards Backing fabric

- Quilt batting, at least 44-inches square

- Rotary cutter, mat, and wide clear-plastic ruler with $1/8$-inch markings are necessary tools in attaining accuracy. A 6 x 24-inch ruler is recommended.

LEAF A

Make 3

Green Print #1, Brown Floral #1, and Orange Plaid fabrics:

Cut one $2^1/2$ x $6^1/2$-inch rectangle.

Cut one $2^1/2$ x $4^1/2$-inch rectangle.

Cut two $2^1/2$-inch squares.

Accessories need not be delegated to just one season. Picnic baskets and a wicker planter take on a double duty when combined with fall foliage, berries, and dried flowers. Earlier in the year, they held summer blooms and vining plants.

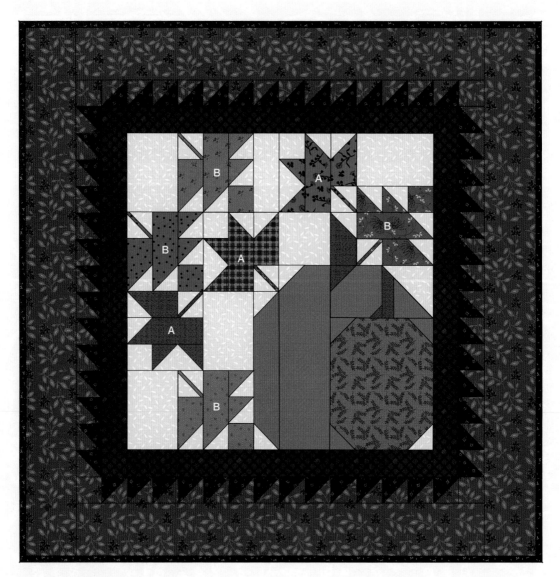

FABRIC KEY

Green Print # 1

Orange Plaid

Brown Print

Black Print

Green Print # 2

Russet Print

Brown Floral #1

Orange Floral

Green Print # 3

Brown Floral #2

Beige Print

Orange Print #1

Orange Print #2

Cut one 1 x 4-inch strip.

Beige Print fabric:
Cut three 2⅝-inch squares.
Cut the squares in half
diagonally.

Cut one 2½ x 42-inch strip.
From this strip cut three
2½ x 4½-inch rectangles,
and cut nine, 2½-inch squares.

PIECING
Step 1
Position a 2½-inch Green #1
square on the corner of a
2½ x 4½-inch Beige rectangle. Draw a diagonal line on
the square and stitch on the
line. Trim the seam allowance
to ¼-inch. Repeat at the other
corner of the rectangle, and
press. Sew a 2½-inch Beige
square to the right-hand side
of this unit, trim, and press.

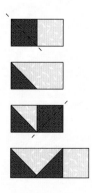

Step 2
Position a 2½-inch Beige
square on the corner of the
2½ x 6½-inch Green #1
rectangle. Draw a diagonal
line on the square and stitch
on the line. Trim the seam
allowance to ¼-inch, and press.

Step 3
Position a 2½-inch Beige
square on the corner of the
2½ x 4½-inch Green #1
rectangle. Draw a diagonal
line on the square and stitch
on the line. Trim the seam
allowance to ¼-inch, and press.

Step 4
To make the Green #1 stem
unit, center a 2⅝-inch Beige
triangle on the 1 x 4-inch
Green strip, as shown. Stitch
a ¼-inch seam, and press.
Repeat on the other side of
the Green strip. Press the
seam allowances toward the
stem. Trim the ends of the
Green stem. At this point the

stem unit should measure
2½-inches square. Sew
the Step 3 unit to the right-
hand side of the stem unit,
and press.

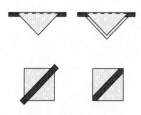

Step 5
Referring to the block diagram, sew together the units
from Step 1, 2, and 4, and
press. At this point Leaf A
should measure 6½-inches
square.

Step 6
For the Brown Floral #1 and
Orange Plaid Leaf A blocks,
repeat Steps 1 through 5.

Leaf B

Make 4

Green Print #2, Green Print #3, Brown Floral #2, and Orange Floral fabrics:

Cut one 2⁷/₈-inch square.

Cut one 2¹/₂ x 6¹/₂-inch rectangle.

Cut one 2¹/₂ x 4¹/₂-inch rectangle.

Cut one 2¹/₂-inch square.

Cut one 1 x 4-inch strip.

Beige Print fabric:

Cut four 2⁷/₈-inch squares.

Cut four 2⁵/₈-inch squares. Cut the squares in half diagonally.

Cut eight 2¹/₂-inch squares.

Piecing

Step 1

Layer together a 2⁷/₈-inch Beige and Orange Floral square. Cut the layered square in half diagonally. Stitch ¹/₄-inch from the diagonal edge of each pair of triangles, and press. Sew the triangle-pieced squares together, then add a 2¹/₂-inch Orange Floral square to the right-hand side of this unit, and press.

Make 2

Step 2

Position a 2¹/₂-inch Beige square on the corner of the 2¹/₂ x 6¹/₂-inch Orange Floral rectangle. Draw a diagonal line on the square and stitch on the line. Trim the seam to ¹/₄-inch, and press.

Step 3

Position a 2¹/₂-inch Beige square on the corner of the 2¹/₂ x 4¹/₂-inch Orange Floral rectangle. Draw a diagonal line on the square and stitch on the line. Trim the seam allowance to ¹/₄-inch and press.

Step 4

To make the Orange Floral stem unit, refer to Leaf A, Step 4. Sew the Step 3 unit to the right-hand side of the stem unit, and press.

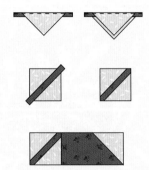

Step 5

Referring to the block diagram, sew together the units from Step 1, 2, and 4, and press. At this point Leaf B should measure 6¹/₂-inches square.

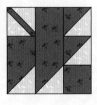

Step 6

For the Green Print #2, Green Print #3, and Brown Floral #2 Leaf B blocks, repeat Steps 1 through 5.

PUMPKINS

Orange Print #1 fabric:
Cut one $8\frac{1}{2}$ x $10\frac{1}{2}$-inch rectangle.

Orange Print #2 fabric:
Cut one $3\frac{7}{8}$ x $4\frac{7}{8}$-inch rectangle.

Cut one $4\frac{1}{2}$ x $14\frac{1}{2}$-inch rectangle.

Cut one $4\frac{1}{2}$-inch square.

Cut one $2\frac{1}{2}$ x $12\frac{1}{2}$-inch rectangle.

Cut three $2\frac{1}{2}$-inch squares.

Beige Print fabric:
Cut one $4\frac{7}{8}$-inch square.

Cut one $4\frac{1}{2}$-inch square.

Cut five $2\frac{1}{2}$-inch squares.

Green Print #1 fabric:
Cut one $2\frac{1}{2}$ x $4\frac{1}{2}$-inch rectangle.

Cut one $2\frac{1}{2}$-inch square.

Cut one $1\frac{1}{2}$ x $4\frac{7}{8}$-inch rectangle.

Cut one $1\frac{1}{2}$-inch square.

PIECING

Step 1

Position three $2\frac{1}{2}$-inch Orange Print #2 squares and one $2\frac{1}{2}$-inch Beige square on the corners of the $8\frac{1}{2}$ x $10\frac{1}{2}$-inch Orange Print #1 rectangle, as shown. Draw diagonal lines on the squares and stitch on these lines. Trim the seam allowances to $\frac{1}{4}$-inch, and press.

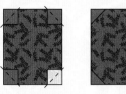

MAKE 1

Step 2

Position two $2\frac{1}{2}$-inch Beige squares on the corners of the $2\frac{1}{2}$ x $12\frac{1}{2}$-inch Orange Print #2 rectangle, as shown. Draw diagonal lines on the squares and stitch on these lines. Trim the seam allowances to $\frac{1}{4}$-inch, and press.

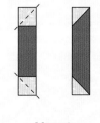

MAKE 1

Step 3

Position a $2\frac{1}{2}$-inch Beige square on the corner of the $4\frac{1}{2}$ x $14\frac{1}{2}$-inch Orange Print #2 rectangle. Draw a diagonal line on the Beige square and stitch on the line. Trim the seam allowance to $\frac{1}{4}$-inch, and press.

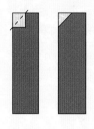

MAKE 1

Step 4

Position a $2\frac{1}{2}$-inch Green #1 square on the corner of the $4\frac{1}{2}$-inch Orange Print #2 square. Draw a diagonal line on the Green square and stitch on the line. Trim the seam allowance to $\frac{1}{4}$-inch, and press. Repeat at the opposite corner of the Orange square with the $1\frac{1}{2}$-inch Green #1 square, as shown.

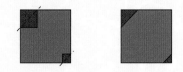

MAKE 1

Step 5

Sew the $1\frac{1}{2}$ x $4\frac{7}{8}$-inch
Green #1 rectangle to
the left-hand side of the
$3\frac{7}{8}$ x $4\frac{7}{8}$-inch Orange Print
#2 rectangle, and press.
Layer the $4\frac{7}{8}$-inch Beige
square on this unit. Cut the
layered square in half diagonally. Stitch a $\frac{1}{4}$-inch seam
along the diagonal edge of
the lower pair of triangles, as
shown, and press. Sew this
unit to the right-hand side of
the Step 4 unit, and press.

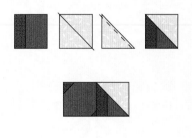

MAKE 1

Step 6

Position a $2\frac{1}{2}$-inch Beige
square on the corner of the
$2\frac{1}{2}$ x $4\frac{1}{2}$-inch Green #1 rectangle. Draw a diagonal line
on the Beige square and
stitch on the line. Trim the
seam allowance to $\frac{1}{4}$-inch,
and press. Sew this unit to
the right-hand side of the
$4\frac{1}{2}$-inch Beige square as
shown, and press.

MAKE 1

QUILT CENTER

Beige Print fabric:
Cut one $4\frac{1}{2}$ x 42-inch strip.
From this strip cut four
$4\frac{1}{2}$ x $6\frac{1}{2}$-inch rectangles,
and cut one $2\frac{1}{2}$ x $6\frac{1}{2}$-inch
rectangle.

QUILT CENTER ASSEMBLY

Referring to the quilt assembly diagram, lay out the leaf
blocks, pumpkin sections,
and beige rectangles. For the
left-hand section, sew the
pieces together in horizontal
rows, and press. Sew the
rows together, and press.
For the right-hand section,
sew the pieces together in
vertical rows, and press.
Sew the sections together,
and press. At this point the
quilt center should measure
$24\frac{1}{2}$-inches square.

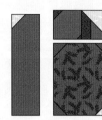

QUILT ASSEMBLY DIAGRAM

BORDERS

*Note: The yardage given allows
for the border strips to be cut on
the crosswise grain.*

Brown Print fabric:
Cut four $2\frac{1}{2}$ x 42-inch strips
for the inner border.

Black Print fabric:
Cut two $2\frac{7}{8}$ x 42-inch strips
for the sawtooth border.

Russet Print fabric:
Cut two $2\frac{7}{8}$ x 42-inch strips
for the sawtooth border.

Cut four $4\frac{1}{2}$ x 42-inch strips
for the outer border.

Cut four $2\frac{1}{2}$-inch squares for
the sawtooth border.

ATTACHING THE BORDERS

Step 1

Measure the quilt from left to right through the center. Cut two 2½-inch wide Brown inner borders to this length. Sew to the top and bottom of the quilt, and press.

Step 2

Measure the quilt top to bottom through the center. Cut two 2½-inch wide Brown inner borders to this length. Sew to the sides of the quilt, and press.

Step 3

To make the sawtooth border, layer the $2\frac{7}{8}$ x 42-inch Black and Russet strips together in pairs. Press them together, but do not sew. Cut the layered strips into squares, as shown, taking care not to shift the layers as you cut.

2⅞"

CROSSCUT 28

Step 4

Cut the squares in half diagonally. Stitch ¼-inch from the diagonal edge of each pair of triangles, and press.

MAKE 56

Step 5

Sew 14 triangle-pieced squares together for each sawtooth border strip, and press. Sew two of the borders to the top and bottom of the quilt, and press.

Step 6

Add 2½-inch Russet squares to both sides of the remaining sawtooth borders, and press. Sew these borders to the sides of the quilt, and press.

Step 7

Measure the quilt from left to right through the center. Cut two 4½-inch wide Russet outer borders to this length. Sew to the top and bottom of the quilt, and press.

Step 8

Measure the quilt from top to bottom through the center.

Cut two 4½-inch wide Russet outer borders to this length and sew to the sides of the quilt, and press.

PUTTING IT ALL TOGETHER

Trim the backing fabric and the batting so they are 4-inches larger than the quilt top dimensions. Mark quilting designs on the quilt top. Layer the backing, batting, and quilt top, and quilt as desired. When quilting is complete, hand baste the three layers together a scant ¼-inch from the quilt top edge. Trim excess batting and backing even with the quilt top.

BINDING

From the binding fabric:
Cut five 2¼ x 42-inch strips.

Sew the binding to the quilt using a ¼-inch seam allowance. This measurement will produce a ⅜-inch wide finished double binding.

BINDING AND DIAGONAL PIECING

See General Instructions on page 140.

Tulips *Tulips*

30 x 40-inches

FABRICS AND SUPPLIES

Yardage is based on 42-inch wide fabric.

- 6 x 12-inch piece each of Six Coordinating Prints for tulips

- 1¼ yards Beige Print for background

- ¼ yard Dark Green Print for stems and corner blocks

- ¼ yard Medium Green Print for leaves

- ⅓ yard Blue Print for checkerboard lattice

- ⅛ yard Red Print for lattice posts and corner blocks

- ½ yard Binding fabric (bias cut)

- 1 yard Backing fabric

- Quilt batting, at least 34 x 44-inches

- Rotary cutter, mat, and wide clear-plastic ruler with ⅛-inch markings are necessary tools in attaining accuracy. A 6 x 24-inch ruler is recommended.

TULIP BLOCKS

Make 6

Six Coordinating Print fabrics:

Cut one 4⅞-inch square. Cut the square in half diagonally for the large triangle for the tulip. You will need only one of these triangles.

Cut one 5¼-inch square. Cut the square diagonally into quarters for the small triangle for the tulip. You will need only one of these triangles.

Beige Print fabric:

Cut two 5¼-inch squares. Cut these squares diagonally into quarters. You will need only six of these triangles for the tulip background.

Bring a fresh touch of spring indoors and create a garden of color and texture. Mix potted plants and fresh cut flowers with a variety of antique and new pottery; here, they are nestled below this charming wallhanging of stitched tulips. The quilt's shades of purple, blue, raspberry, and gold on a background of sun dappled beige are a perfect way to bring the long-awaited spring indoors.

FABRIC KEY

Coordinating Print   Beige Print   Dark Green Print   Medium Green Print   Blue Print   Red Print

Cut twelve 2-inch squares for the leaf background.

Cut three 2½ x 42-inch strips. From these strips cut twelve 2½ x 8½-inch rectangles for the flower background.

Dark Green Print fabric:
Cut six 1½ x 4½-inch rectangles for the stems.

Medium Green Print fabric:
Cut two 2 x 42-inch strips. From these strips cut twelve 2 x 4½-inch rectangles for the leaves.

PIECING
Step 1
Sew the Beige triangles to each of the six coordinating print small triangles along a bias edge, and press. Sew a corresponding print large triangle to each of these units, and press.

MAKE 1

Step 2
Position a 2-inch Beige square at the corner of a 2 x 4½-inch Medium Green rectangle. Draw a diagonal line on the Beige square and stitch on the line. Trim the seam allowance to ¼-inch, and press. Repeat this process for the remaining 2 x 4½-inch Medium Green rectangles, following the directions of the stitching lines.

MAKE 6 LEFT-HAND LEAF UNITS
MAKE 6 RIGHT-HAND LEAF UNITS

Step 3
Sew the leaf units to both sides of the 1½ x 4½-inch Dark Green rectangles, and press. Sew the Step 1 flower units to the top of the stem/leaf units, and press. Sew a 2½ x 8½-inch Beige rectangle to both sides of each flower, and press. At this point, the flower block should measure 8½-inches square.

MAKE 1 FLOWER BLOCK
FROM EACH PRINT

QUILT CENTER

Blue Print fabric:
Cut five 1½ x 42-inch strips for the checkerboard lattice.

Beige Print fabric:
Cut five 1½ x 42-inch strips for the checkerboard lattice.

Red Print fabric:
Cut one 2½ x 42-inch strip. From this strip cut twelve, 2½-inch squares for the lattice posts and cut four 2½-inch squares for the corner blocks to be used in the border.

QUILT CENTER ASSEMBLY
Step 1
Sew the 1½ x 42-inch Blue and Beige strips together in pairs, and press. Make a total of five strip sets. Cut the strip sets into segments.

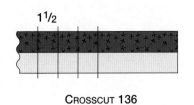

1½

CROSSCUT 136

Step 2

Sew eight Step 1 segments together for each lattice strip, and press.

MAKE 17

Step 3

Sew together three Step 2 lattice strips and four $2\frac{1}{2}$-inch Red lattice posts, and press.

MAKE 3

Step 4

Sew together four Step 2 lattice strips and three flower blocks, and press. Repeat this process with the remaining lattice strips and flower blocks. Sew the Step 3 and Step 4 units together, and press. At this point, the quilt center should measure $22\frac{1}{2}$ x $32\frac{1}{2}$-inches.

BORDERS

Note: The yardage given allows for the borders to be cut on the crosswise grain.

Beige Print fabric:

Cut one $2\frac{7}{8}$ x 14-inch strip for the triangle-pieced squares for the corner blocks.

Cut two $2\frac{1}{2}$ x $18\frac{1}{2}$-inch strips for the side inner border.

Cut two $2\frac{1}{2}$ x $28\frac{1}{2}$-inch strips for the top and bottom inner border.

Cut two $2\frac{1}{2}$ x $30\frac{1}{2}$-inch strips for the side outer border.

Cut two $2\frac{1}{2}$ x $36\frac{1}{2}$-inch strips for the top and bottom outer border.

Dark Green Print fabric:

Cut one $2\frac{7}{8}$ x 14-inch strip for the triangle-pieced squares for the corner blocks.

ATTACHING THE BORDERS

Step 1

Layer the $2\frac{7}{8}$ x 14-inch Beige and Dark Green strips, and press. Cut the strips into $2\frac{7}{8}$-inch squares, taking care not to shift the layers as you cut.

$2\frac{7}{8}$

CROSSCUT 4

Step 2

Cut the layered squares in half diagonally. Stitch $\frac{1}{4}$-inch from the diagonal edge of each pair of triangles, and press. At this point each triangle-pieced square should measure $2\frac{1}{2}$-inches square.

MAKE 8

Step 3

Sew a triangle-pieced square to both ends of the $2\frac{1}{2}$ x $28\frac{1}{2}$-inch Beige strips, and press. Sew these inner borders to the top and bottom edges of the quilt center, and press.

Step 4

Sew a triangle-pieced square to both ends of the $2\frac{1}{2}$ x $18\frac{1}{2}$-inch Beige strips. Add a $2\frac{1}{2}$-inch Red corner square to both ends of the strips, and press. Sew these inner borders to the sides of the quilt center, and press.

Step 5

Sew the 2½ x 36½-inch Beige outer border strips to the top and bottom of the quilt center, and press. Sew the 2½ x 30½-inch Beige outer border strips to the sides of the quilt center, and press.

PUTTING IT ALL TOGETHER

Step 1

Trim the backing fabric and batting so they are 2-inches larger than the quilt top dimensions.

Step 2

Mark quilting designs on the quilt top. Layer the backing, batting, and quilt top, and quilt as desired. When quilting is complete, hand baste the three layers together a scant ¼-inch from the quilt top edge. Trim excess batting and backing even with the quilt top.

BIAS BINDING

From the binding fabric:

Cut enough 2¾-inch wide bias strips to make a strip 160-inches long. Sew the binding to the quilt using a ⅜-inch seam allowance. This measurement will produce a ½-inch wide finished double binding.

BINDING AND DIAGONAL PIECING

See General Instructions on page 140.

Star *Patch*

24-inches square

FABRICS AND SUPPLIES
Yardage is based on 42-inch wide fabric.

- 1/4 yard Black Print for Nine-Patch blocks

- 1/4 yard Beige Print for Nine-Patch blocks and background

- 1/4 yard Gold Print for outer star

- 1/4 yard Red Print #1 for center star

- 1/2 yard Red Print #2 for border

- 1/3 yard Binding fabric

- 7/8 yard Backing fabric

- Quilt batting, at least 28-inches square

- Rotary cutter, mat and wide clear-plastic ruler with 1/8-inch markings are neces-sary tools in obtaining accu-racy. A 6 x 24-inch ruler is recommended.

NINE-PATCH BLOCKS
Make 4

Black Print fabric:
Cut two 2 1/2 x 21-inch strips.

Cut one 2 1/2 x 12-inch strip.

Beige Print fabric:
Cut one 2 1/2 x 21-inch strip.

Cut two 2 1/2 x 12-inch strips.

PIECING
Step 1
Sew 2 1/2 x 21-inch Black strips to both sides of the 2 1/2 x 21-inch Beige strip, and press. Cut the strip set into segments.

2 1/2"

CROSSCUT 8

The easy yet bold quilt design makes a dramatic decorating statement on the panelled wall.

Use paint to update dark, dated paneling. Wash the paneling with TSP (trisodium-phosphate, available at hardware stores), then sand the panel surface to a dull glossy finish. Prime and paint.

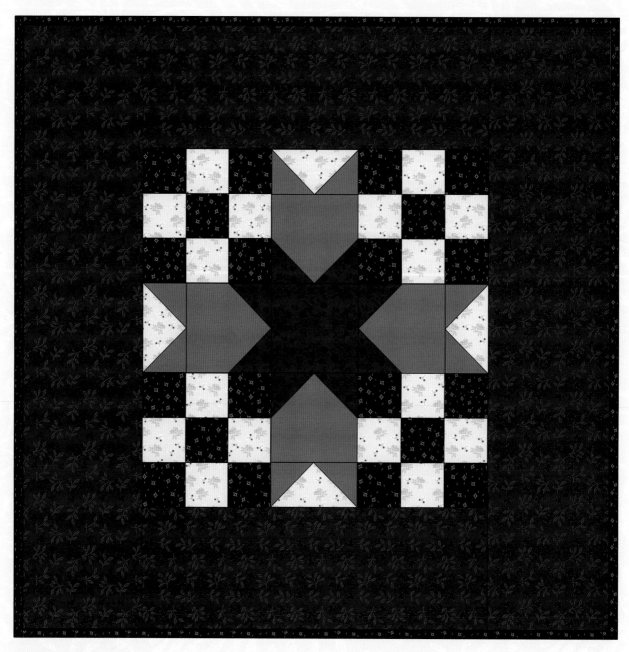

FABRIC KEY

Black Print

Beige Print

Gold Print

Red Print # 1

Red Print # 2

Step 2

Sew 2½ x 12-inch Beige strips to both sides of the 2½ x 12-inch Black strip, and press. Cut the strip set into segments.

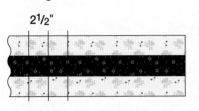

CROSSCUT 4

Step 3

Sew the Step 1 segments to both sides of the Step 2 segments, and press.

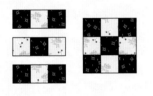

MAKE 4

STAR

Gold Print fabric:

Cut four 4½-inch squares.

Cut eight 2½-inch squares.

Beige Print fabric:

Cut four 2½ x 4½-inch rectangles.

Red Print #1 fabric:

Cut one 4½-inch square.

Cut eight 2½-inch squares.

PIECING

Step 1

Position a 2½-inch Gold square on the corner of a 2½ x 4½-inch Beige rectangle. Draw a diagonal line on the Gold square and stitch on the line. Trim the seam allowance to ¼-inch, and press. Repeat this process at the opposite corner of the Beige rectangle.

MAKE 4

Step 2

Position a 2½-inch Red #1 square on the corner of a 4½-inch Gold square. Draw a diagonal line on the Red square and stitch on the line. Trim the seam allowance to ¼-inch, and press. Repeat this process on the adjacent corner of the Gold square.

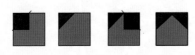

MAKE 4

Step 3

Sew the Step 1 and Step 2 units together in pairs, and press.

MAKE 4

Step 4

Sew Step 3 units to both sides of the 4½-inch Red #1 square, and press.

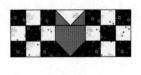

MAKE 1

Step 5

Sew Nine-Patch blocks to both sides of the remaining Step 3 units, and press.

MAKE 2

Step 6

Sew the Step 5 units to both sides of the Step 4 unit, and press.

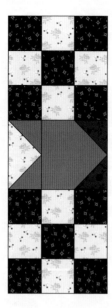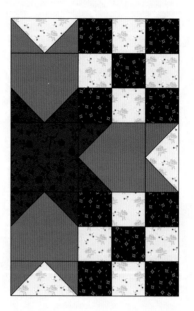

BORDER

Note: The yardage given allows for the border strips to be cut on the crosswise grain.

Red Print #2 fabric:

Cut three $4^{1}/_{2}$ x 42-inch strips for the outer border.

ATTACHING THE BORDER

Step 1

Measure the quilt from left to right through the center. Cut two $4^{1}/_{2}$-inch wide Red #2 border strips to this measurement. Sew the border strips to the top and bottom of the quilt, and press.

Step 2

Measure the quilt from top to bottom through the center. Cut two $4^{1}/_{2}$-inch wide Red #2 border strips to this measurement. Sew the border strips to the sides of the quilt, and press.

PUTTING IT ALL TOGETHER

Step 1

Trim the backing fabric and batting so they are 4-inches larger than the quilt top dimensions.

Step 2

Mark quilting designs on the quilt top. Layer the backing, batting, and quilt top, and quilt as desired. When quilting is complete, hand baste the three layers together a scant $^{1}/_{4}$-inch from the quilt top edge. Trim excess batting and backing even with the quilt top.

BINDING

From the binding fabric:

Cut three $2^{1}/_{4}$ x 42-inch strips.

Sew the binding to the quilt using a $^{1}/_{4}$-inch seam allowance. This measurement will produce a $^{3}/_{8}$-inch wide finished double binding.

BINDING AND DIAGONAL PIECING

See General Instructions on page 140.

A Welcoming Touch...

An empty wall can be brightened instantly with a cozy vignette consisting of a quilt, side table, and a seasonal floral or fruit arrangement. The larger the space, the larger the quilt needed.

Small quilts framed behind glass offer a wonderful handmade touch, yet are protected and under a surface that can be cleaned. Consider a grouping of framed quilt blocks as the solution for a plain wall in the eating area.

Hide-Away

20-inches square

FABRICS AND SUPPLIES

Yardage is based on 42-inch wide fabric.

- $1/3$ yard Beige Print for background and fence

- $1/8$ yard Brown Print for birdhouse, checkerboard, and corner squares

- $3/8$ yard Black Print for checkerboard, roof, hole, and binding

- $1/4$ yard Tan Print for middle border and fence background

- $1/4$ yard Red Print for inner border and outer border

- $2/3$ yard Backing fabric

- $2^{1}/_{2}$-inch square of light-weight cardboard

- Quilt batting, at least 24-inches square

- Rotary cutter, mat and wide clear-plastic ruler with $1/8$-inch markings are necessary tools in obtaining accuracy. A 6 x 24-inch ruler is recommended.

BIRDHOUSE BLOCK

Brown Print fabric:
Cut one $2^{1}/_{2}$ x $6^{1}/_{2}$-inch rectangle.

Cut two $2^{1}/_{2}$-inch squares.

Cut six $1^{1}/_{2}$-inch squares.

Black Print fabric:
Cut one $4^{7}/_{8}$-inch square.

Cut six $1^{1}/_{2}$-inch squares.

Cut one $2^{1}/_{2}$-inch square.

Beige Print fabric:
Cut one $4^{7}/_{8}$-inch square.

Cut two $1^{1}/_{2}$ x $4^{1}/_{2}$-inch rectangles.

Add the charm of an old-fashioned cottage to a room's interior by giving the walls a creamy white coat of paint. Collect a mix of furniture—great garage-sale finds create interesting combinations. A fresh coat of paint can coordinate many different styles.

FABRIC KEY

Beige Print

Brown Print

Black Print

Tan Print

Red Print

PIECING

Step 1

Layer the 4⅞-inch Beige and Black squares. Cut the layered squares in half diagonally. Stitch ¼-inch from the diagonal edge of each pair of triangles, and press.

MAKE 2

Step 2

Position 2½-inch Brown squares on the triangle-pieced squares as shown in the diagram. Draw a diagonal line on each square and stitch on the line. Trim the seam allowance to ¼-inch, and press. Sew the two units together to form the roof section.

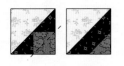

MAKE 2

Step 3

Referring to the quilt diagram, sew the 1½-inch Brown and Black squares together to form the checkerboard, and press. Sew this unit to the 2½ x 6½-inch Brown rectangle to form the house base section. Sew the 1½ x 4½-inch Beige rectangles to both sides of the base section, and press.

Step 4

Sew the Step 2 roof section to the top of the Step 3 house base section, and press.

Step 5

Cut out a 1¾-inch diameter circle from the lightweight cardboard. With this appliqué method, the cardboard forms the base around which the birdhouse hole is shaped. This technique helps you to create smooth, well-rounded circles.

BIRDHOUSE HOLE

Cut 1 out of lightweight cardboard.

Step 6

Position the cardboard template on the wrong side of the 2½-inch Black square, and trace. Cut a scant ¼-inch beyond the drawn line.

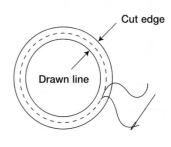

Cut edge

Drawn line

Step 7

Run gathering stitches halfway between the drawn line and the cut edge of the circle. The thread ends should be about 3-inches longer than needed.

Step 8

Position the cardboard template on the wrong side of the fabric circle, and pull up the gathering stitches. Once the thread is tight, space the gathering evenly, knot the thread, and press. Remove the cardboard template. Position the fabric circle on the birdhouse, and appliqué it in place using matching thread.

BORDERS

Note: The yardage given allows for the border strips to be cut on the crosswise grain.

Red Print fabric:

Cut one $1\frac{1}{2}$ x 42-inch strip for the inner border.

Cut two $2\frac{1}{2}$ x 42-inch strips for the outer border.

Tan Print fabric:

Cut two $1\frac{1}{2}$ x 42-inch strips for the middle border.

Cut two $1\frac{1}{2}$ x 42-inch strips. From these strips cut forty eight, $1\frac{1}{2}$-inch squares for the fence background.

Beige Print fabric:

Cut two $2\frac{1}{2}$ x 42-inch strips. From these strips cut twenty four, $2\frac{1}{2}$-inch squares for the fence border.

Brown Print fabric:

Cut eight $2\frac{1}{2}$-inch corner squares.

ATTACHING THE BORDERS

Step 1

Measure the block from left to right through the center. Cut two $1\frac{1}{2}$-inch wide Red border strips to this measurement. Sew the border strips to the top and bottom of the block, and press.

Step 2

Measure the block from top to bottom through the center. Cut two $1\frac{1}{2}$-inch wide Red border strips to this measurement. Sew the border strips to the sides of the block, and press.

Step 3

Measure the quilt from left to right through the center. Cut two $1\frac{1}{2}$-inch wide Tan border strips to this measurement. Sew the border strips to the top and bottom of the quilt, and press.

Step 4

Measure the quilt from top to bottom through the center. Cut two $1\frac{1}{2}$-inch wide Tan border strips to this measurement. Sew the border strips to the sides of the quilt, and press.

Step 5

Position $1\frac{1}{2}$-inch Tan corner square on one corner of each $2\frac{1}{2}$-inch Beige square. Draw a diagonal line on the squares and stitch on the line. Trim the seam allowances to $1/4$-inch, and press. Repeat this process for the adjacent corner of the $2\frac{1}{2}$-inch Beige squares.

MAKE 24

Step 6

Sew six of the fence units together for each border, and press. Sew fence borders to the top and bottom of the quilt, and press.

Step 7

Add $2\frac{1}{2}$-inch Brown corner squares to both ends of the remaining fence borders, and press. Sew these borders to the sides of the quilt, and press.

Step 8

Measure the quilt from left to right through the center. Cut two $2\frac{1}{2}$-inch wide Red border strips to this measurement. Sew the border strips to the top and bottom of the quilt, and press.

Step 9

Cut two more, $2\frac{1}{2}$-inch wide Red border strips to the above measurement for the side borders. Add $2\frac{1}{2}$-inch Brown corner squares to both sides of the strips, and press. Sew the border strips to the sides of the quilt, and press.

PUTTING IT ALL TOGETHER

Step 1

Trim the batting and backing so they are 4-inches larger than the quilt top dimensions.

Step 2

Mark quilting designs on the quilt top. Layer the backing, batting, and quilt top, and quilt as desired. When quilting is complete, hand baste the three layers together a scant $\frac{1}{4}$-inch from the quilt top edge. Trim excess batting and backing even with the quilt top.

BINDING

From the binding fabric:

Cut three $2\frac{1}{4}$ x 42-inch strips.

Sew the binding to the quilt using a $\frac{1}{4}$-inch seam allowance. This measurement will produce a $\frac{3}{8}$-inch wide finished double binding.

BINDING AND DIAGONAL PIECING

See General Instructions on page 140.

A *Welcoming* Touch...

For a harmonious grouping, pull together different objects with similar colors. Although textures may vary, the color will unify the elements.

Fireworks

60-inches square

FABRICS AND SUPPLIES

Yardage is based on 42-inch wide fabric.

- 1 yard Gold Print for stars, lattice posts, and middle border

- 1¼ yards Blue Print for star background, center square, corner squares, and pieced border

- 1¾ yards Red Print for lattice strips, pieced and outer border

- 1 yard Blue Plaid for lattice strips and inner border

- ¾ yard Binding fabric (bias cut)

- 3½ yards Backing fabric

- Quilt batting, at least 64-inches square

- Rotary cutter, mat and wide clear-plastic ruler with

⅛-inch markings are necessary tools in attaining accuracy. A 6 x 24-inch ruler is recommended.

STAR BLOCKS

Make 4

Gold Print fabric:

Cut one 4½ x 42-inch strip. From this strip cut four 4½-inch squares.

Cut four 2½ x 42-inch strips. From these strips cut sixty four 2½-inch squares.

Blue Print fabric:

Cut two 4½ x 42-inch strips. From these strips cut sixteen 4½-inch squares.

Cut four 2½ x 42-inch strips. From these strips cut thirty two 2½ x 4½-inch rectangles.

A graphic quilt can serve as a focal point in a room, just as a large piece of artwork would do.

The combination of deep blues, cranberry, and rich gold contrast nicely with the white-washed pine walls.

FABRIC KEY

Gold Print

Blue Print

Red Print

Blue Plaid

PIECING
Step 1
Position a 2½-inch Gold square on the corner of a 2½ x 4½-inch Blue rectangle. Draw a diagonal line on the Gold square and stitch on the line. Trim the seam allowance to ¼-inch, and press. Repeat this process at the opposite corner of the Blue rectangle.

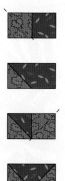

MAKE 32

Step 2
Sew the Step 1 units together in pairs, and press. Sew eight pairs to the top and bottom of the 4½-inch Gold squares, and press.

MAKE 4

Step 3
Sew 4½-inch Blue squares to the sides of the remaining eight Step 2 pairs, and press. Sew these units to the sides of the star block, and press. At this point the blocks should measure 12½-inches square.

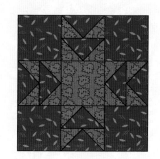

MAKE 4

QUILT CENTER

Red Print fabric:
Cut seven 2½ x 42-inch strips. From these strips cut sixteen 2½ x 12½-inch lattice strips, and cut eight 2½ x 4½-inch lattice strips.

Blue Plaid fabric:
Cut six 4½ x 42-inch strips. From these strips cut four 4½ x 12½-inch lattice strips, and cut four 4½ x 36½-inch inner border strips.

Gold Print fabric:
Cut one 2½ x 42-inch strip. From this strip cut sixteen 2½-inch square lattice posts.

Blue Print fabric:
Cut one 4½ x 42-inch strip. From this strip cut five 4½-inch squares for the center square and the corner squares.

QUILT CENTER ASSEMBLY
Step 1
Sew together two star blocks, four 2½ x 12½-inch Red lattice strips, and one 4½ x 12½-inch Blue Plaid lattice strip, and press.

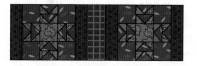

MAKE 2

Step 2
Sew together two 2½ x 12½-inch Red lattice strips, one 2½ x 4½-inch Red lattice strip, and four 2½-inch Gold lattice posts, and press.

MAKE 4

Step 3
Sew together four 2½ x 4½-inch Red lattice strips, two 4½ x 12½-inch Blue Plaid lattice strips, and one

4½-inch Blue Print square, and press.

MAKE 1

Step 4
Referring to the quilt diagram, sew together the Step 1, 2, and 3 units, and press.

Step 5
Sew the 4½ x 36½-inch Blue Plaid inner border strips to the top and bottom of the quilt center, and press.

Step 6
Add 4½-inch Blue Print corner squares to both ends of the remaining 4½ x 36½-inch Blue Plaid inner border strips, and press. Sew these strips to the sides of the quilt, and press.

BORDERS
Note: The yardage given allows for the border strips to be cut on the crosswise grain. Diagonally piece the strips together as needed.

Gold Print fabric:
Cut five 2½ x 42-inch strips for the middle border.

Red Print fabric:
Cut six 2½ x 42-inch strips. From these strips cut two 2½ x 32½-inch strips, cut two 2½ x 28½-inch strips, cut two 2½ x 6½-inch rectangles, cut twelve 2½ x 4½-inch rectangles, and cut six 2½-inch squares for the pieced border.

Cut five 4½ x 42-inch strips. From these strips cut four 4½ x 48½-inch outer border strips.

Blue Print fabric:
Cut one 6½ x 42-inch strip. From this strip cut four 6½-inch corner squares.

Cut two 2½ x 42-inch strips. From these strips cut twenty, 2½-inch squares for the pieced border.

PIECING AND ATTACHING THE BORDERS
Step 1
Measure the quilt from top to bottom through the center. Cut two 2½-inch wide Gold middle borders to this measurement. Sew the strips to the sides of the quilt, and press.

Step 2
Measure the quilt from left to right through the center, including the borders just added. Cut two 2½-inch wide Gold middle borders to this measurement. Sew the strips to the top and bottom of the quilt, and press.

Step 3
Position a 2½-inch Blue square on the corner of a 2½ x 4½-inch Red rectangle. Draw a diagonal line on the Blue square and stitch on the line. Trim the seam allowance to ¼-inch, and press. Repeat this process at the opposite corner of the Red rectangle.

MAKE 10

Step 4
For the top and bottom pieced borders, sew together three Step 3 units, two 2½-inch Red squares, one 2½ x 4½-inch Red rectangle,

and one $2\frac{1}{2}$ x $28\frac{1}{2}$-inch Red strip, and press. Add a $4\frac{1}{2}$ x $48\frac{1}{2}$-inch Red outer border strip to this unit and press. Sew these borders to the top and the bottom of the quilt and press.

MAKE 2

Step 5

For the side pieced borders, sew together two Step 3 units, one $2\frac{1}{2}$-inch Red square, one $2\frac{1}{2}$ x $6\frac{1}{2}$-inch Red rectangle, and one $2\frac{1}{2}$ x $32\frac{1}{2}$-inch Red strip, and press. Add a $4\frac{1}{2}$ x $48\frac{1}{2}$-inch Red outer border strip to this unit and press.

MAKE 2

Step 6

Sew $6\frac{1}{2}$-inch Blue Print corner squares to both ends of the borders from Step 5, and press. Sew borders to the sides of the quilt, and press.

PUTTING IT ALL TOGETHER

Step 1

Cut the $3\frac{1}{2}$-yard length of backing in half crosswise to make two $1\frac{3}{4}$-yard lengths. Sew the two lengths together along the long edge. Trim the backing fabric and batting so they are about 4-inches larger than the quilt top dimensions.

Step 2

Mark quilting designs on the quilt top. Layer the backing, batting, and quilt top, and quilt as desired. When quilting is complete, hand baste the three layers together a scant $\frac{1}{4}$-inch from the quilt top edge. Trim excess batting and backing even with the quilt top.

BIAS BINDING

From the binding fabric:

Cut enough $2\frac{3}{4}$-inch wide bias strips to make a strip 250-inches long. Join the bias strips with diagonal seams. Sew the binding to the quilt using a $\frac{3}{8}$-inch seam allowance. This measurement will produce a $\frac{1}{2}$-inch wide finished double binding.

BINDING AND DIAGONAL PIECING INSTRUCTIONS

See General Instructions on page 140.

Oak Leaf *Basket*

24 x 28-inches

FABRICS AND SUPPLIES

Yardage is based on 42-inch wide fabric.

- $3/8$ yard Green Print for basket

- $1/2$ yard Beige Print for background

- $1/8$ yard Cream Print for fence

- $1/3$ yard Gold Print for inner border

- $1/8$ yard Black Print for corner squares

- $1/3$ yard Brown Print for outer border

- A fat quarter of six Coordinating Prints for leaf and berry appliqués

- $1/2$ yard paper-backed fusible web for appliqués

- #8 Black and Gold pearl cotton thread

- $1/4$ yard Binding fabric

- $7/8$ yard Backing fabric

- Quilt batting, at least 28 x 32-inches

- Rotary cutter, mat, and wide clear-plastic ruler with $1/8$-inch markings are necessary tools in attaining accuracy. A 6 x 24-inch ruler is recommended.

BASKET BLOCK

Green Print fabric:

Cut one $5^{1}/4$-inch square. Cut this square into quarters diagonally. You will be using only two of the small triangles.

Cut one $4^{7}/8$-inch square. Cut this square in half diagonally to form two large triangles.

Cut one 2 x 17-inch long bias strip.

A *small wall quilt that is quick and easy to make can make a dramatic decorating statement with rich colors and simple shapes.*

A *quilt that hints of a particular season is a nice backdrop for other seasonal collectibles.*

FABRIC KEY

Green Print

Beige Print

Cream Print

Gold Print

Black Print

Brown Print

Beige Print fabric:

Cut one 5¼-inch square. Cut this square into quarters diagonally. You will be using only two of the triangles.

Cut one 7½ x 8½-inch rectangle.

Cut two 3½ x 12½-inch rectangles.

Cut one 1½ x 8½-inch rectangle.

PIECING

Step 1

Sew a small Beige and Green triangle together along a bias edge as shown, and press. Sew a large Green triangle to this unit, and press.

MAKE 1

Step 2

Sew a small Beige and Green triangle together along the opposite bias edge as shown, and press. Sew a large Green triangle to this unit and press.

MAKE 1

Step 3

Sew together the Step 1 and Step 2 units, and press.

Step 4

Fold the 2 x 17-inch Green bias strip in half lengthwise, wrong sides together and press. To keep the raw edges aligned, stitch ¼-inch away from the raw edges. Fold the strip in half again so the raw edges are hidden by the first folded edge, and press.

Step 5

Using the Handle Placement Diagram on page 64 as a guide, position and pin the Green bias strip to the 7½ x 8½-inch Beige rectangle. With matching thread, hand appliqué the handle in place.

Step 6

Sew the Step 5 handle unit to the Step 3 basket unit, and press. Sew the 1½ x 8½-inch Beige rectangle to the bottom of the basket, and sew the 3½ x 12½-inch Beige rectangles to the sides of the basket and press.

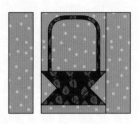

FENCE SECTIONS

Make 2

Cream Print fabric:

Cut one 2½ x 42-inch strip. From this strip cut ten 2½ x 3½-inch rectangles.

Cut one 1½ x 15-inch strip.

Beige Print fabric:

Cut two $1\frac{1}{2}$ x 15-inch strips.

Cut one $1\frac{1}{2}$ x 42-inch strip. From this strip cut twenty $1\frac{1}{2}$-inch squares.

PIECING

Step 1

Sew the $1\frac{1}{2}$ x 15-inch Beige strips to both sides of the $1\frac{1}{2}$ x 15-inch Cream strip, and press. Cut into segments.

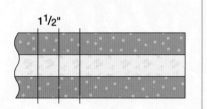

$1\frac{1}{2}$"

CROSSCUT 8

Step 2

Position a $1\frac{1}{2}$-inch Beige square on the corner of a $2\frac{1}{2}$ x $3\frac{1}{2}$-inch Cream rectangle. Draw a diagonal line on the Beige square and stitch on the line. Trim the seam allowances to $\frac{1}{4}$-inch, and press. Repeat this process at the adjacent corner.

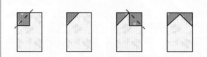

MAKE 10

Step 3

Sew together four Step 1 units and five Step 2 units, and press. Sew the fence sections to the top and bottom of the quilt center, and press.

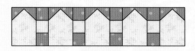

MAKE 2

BORDERS

Note: The yardage given allows for the border strips to be cut on the crosswise grain.

Gold Print fabric:

Cut two $3\frac{1}{2}$ x 42-inch strips for the inner border.

Black Print fabric:

Cut four $3\frac{1}{2}$-inch corner squares.

Brown Print fabric:

Cut three $2\frac{1}{2}$ x 42-inch strips for the outer border.

ATTACHING THE BORDERS

Step 1

Measure the quilt from left to right through the center. Cut two $3\frac{1}{2}$-inch wide Gold inner border strips to this measurement. Sew the strips to the top and bottom of the quilt, and press.

Step 2

Measure the quilt from top to bottom including seam allowances, but not the borders just added. Cut two $3\frac{1}{2}$-inch wide Gold inner border strips to this measurement. Add $3\frac{1}{2}$-inch Black corner squares to the ends of these strips, and press. Sew the strips to the sides of the quilt, and press.

Step 3

Measure the quilt from left to right through the center. Cut two $2\frac{1}{2}$-inch wide Brown outer border strips to this measurement. Sew the strips to the top and bottom of the quilt, and press.

Step 4

Measure the quilt from top to bottom through the center. Cut two 2$\frac{1}{2}$-inch wide Brown outer border strips to this measurement. Sew the strips to the sides of the quilt, and press.

FUSIBLE WEB APPLIQUÉ

The appliqué patterns are on page 64.

Step 1

Trace the templates on the paper side of the fusible web, taking care to leave $\frac{1}{2}$-inch between shapes. Cut apart, leaving a small margin beyond the drawn lines.

Step 2

Following the manufacturer's instructions, apply the fusible web shapes to the wrong side of the selected fabrics. Let cool and cut on the traced lines. Remove the paper backing.

Step 3

Referring to the quilt diagram, position the appliqués on the quilt top and fuse in place.

Step 4

Using one strand of pearl cotton, buttonhole stitch around these shapes.

BUTTONHOLE STITCH

PUTTING IT ALL TOGETHER

Step 1

Trim the backing fabric and batting so they are 4-inches larger than the quilt top dimensions.

Step 2

Mark quilting designs on the quilt top. Layer the backing, batting, and quilt top, and quilt as desired. When quilting is complete, band baste the three layers together a scant $\frac{1}{4}$-inch from the quilt top edge. Trim excess batting and backing even with the quilt top.

BINDING

From the binding fabric:

Cut three 2$\frac{1}{4}$ x 42-inch strips. Sew the binding to the quilt using a $\frac{1}{4}$-inch seam allowance. This measurement will produce a finished $\frac{3}{8}$-inch wide finished double binding.

BINDING AND DIAGONAL PIECING

See General Instructions on page 140.

The appliqué shapes are reversed for tracing purposes. They will appear in the correct position when traced onto fusible web.

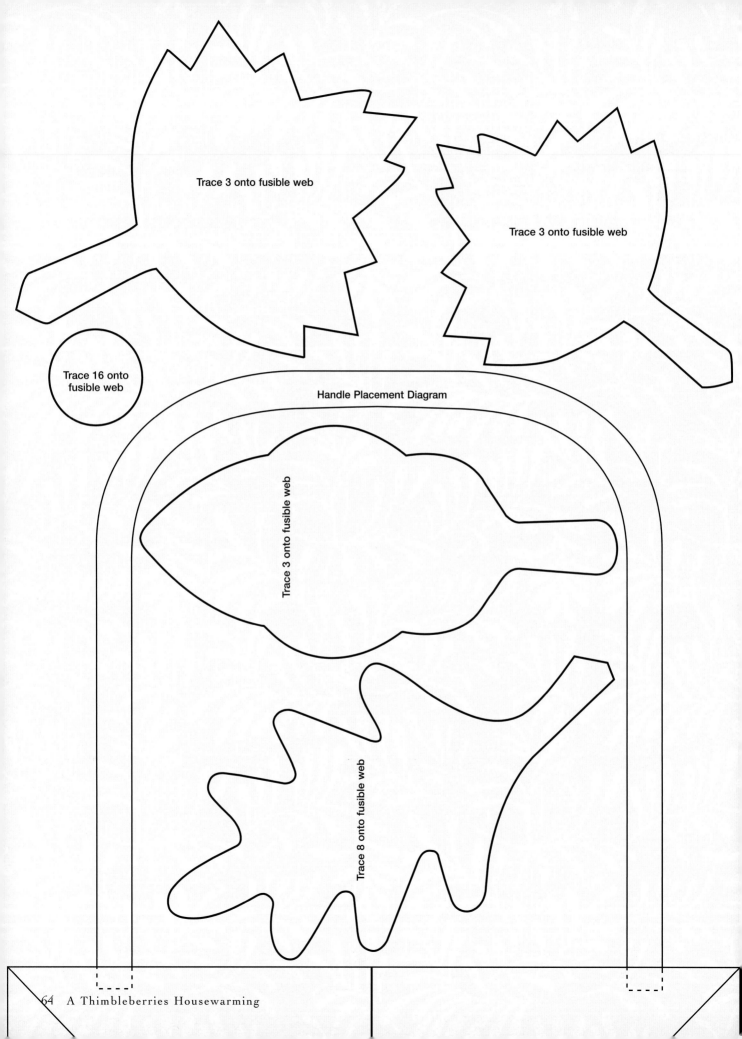

Trace 3 onto fusible web

Trace 3 onto fusible web

Trace 16 onto
fusible web

Handle Placement Diagram

Trace 3 onto fusible web

Trace 8 onto fusible web

These patchwork hearts combined with rich greens and a striking plaid border turn a corner of the house into a special spot for a cup of tea, or perhaps a place to browse through a stack of cookbooks. The design is classic and extends far beyond Valentine's Day. "Be Mine" is a perfect gift—an expression of love and caring that can be enjoyed year round.

40-inches square

FABRICS AND SUPPLIES

Yardage is based on 42-inch wide fabric.

- $1/4$ yard each of Three Red Prints for hearts

- $1/4$ yard Green Print #1 for Nine-Patch blocks

- $1/3$ yard Beige Print for background

- $1/2$ yard Green Print #2 for lattice and inner border

- $3/4$ yard Red Plaid for outer border

- $1/4$ yard Green Print #3 for corner squares

- $1/2$ yard Binding fabric

- $1 1/4$ yards Backing fabric

- Quilt batting, at least 44-inches square

- Rotary cutter, mat and wide clear-plastic ruler with $1/8$-inch markings are necessary tools for attaining accuracy. A 6 x 24-inch ruler is recommended.

HEART BLOCKS

Make 12

Three Red Print fabrics:
Cut one $4 1/2$ x 42-inch strip. From this strip cut four $4 1/2$ x $6 1/2$-inch rectangles, and four $2 1/2$ x $4 1/2$-inch rectangles.

Beige Print fabric:
Cut one $2 1/2$ x 42-inch strip. From this strip cut twelve $2 1/2$-inch squares.

Cut two $1 1/2$ x 42-inch strips. From these strips cut forty eight $1 1/2$-inch squares.

FABRIC KEY

Red Print #1

Red Print #2

Red Print #3

Green Print # 1

Beige Print

Green Print # 2

Red Plaid

Green Print # 3

PIECING

Step 1

Position 1½-inch Beige squares at the upper corners of the 2½ x 4½-inch Red #1 rectangle. Draw a diagonal line on the Beige squares and stitch on the line. Trim the seam allowances to ¼-inch, and press. Sew a 2½-inch Beige square to the right-hand edge of this unit, and press.

MAKE 4

Step 2

Repeat this process for the 2½ x 4½-inch Red #2 and Red #3 rectangles. Sew a 2½-inch Beige square to the right-hand edge of each of these units, and press.

MAKE 4   MAKE 4

Step 3

Position 1½-inch Beige squares at the upper corners of the 4½ x 6½-inch Red #1 rectangle. Draw a diagonal line on the Beige squares and stitch on the line. Trim the

seam allowance to ¼-inch, and press. Repeat this process for the remaining Red #1, Red #2, and Red #3 rectangles. Sew the corresponding units from Steps 1 and 2 to the left-hand side of each of these units, and press.

MAKE 4 HEARTS FROM EACH
RED FABRIC

NINE-PATCH BLOCKS

Make 4

Green Print #1 fabric:

Cut two 2½ x 12-inch strips.

Cut one 2½ x 21-inch strip.

Beige Print fabric:

Cut one 2½ x 12-inch strip.

Cut two 2½ x 21-inch strips.

PIECING

Step 1

Sew the 2½ x 12-inch Green #1 strips to both sides of the 2½ x 12-inch Beige strip, and press. Cut the strip set into segments.

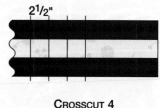

CROSSCUT 4

Step 2

Sew the 2½ x 21-inch Beige strips to both sides of the 2½ x 21-inch Green #1 strip, and press. Cut the strip set into segments.

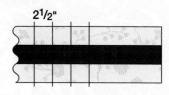

CROSSCUT 8

Step 3

Sew the Step 2 units to both sides of the Step 1 units, and press.

MAKE 4

QUILT CENTER

Green Print #2 fabric:

Cut three 2½ x 26½-inch strips for lattice and top and bottom inner borders.

Cut two 2½ x 30½-inch strips for side inner borders.

Cut two 2½ x 12½-inch strips for lattice.

QUILT CENTER ASSEMBLY

Step 1

Referring to the block diagram, sew the heart blocks and Nine-Patch blocks together, and press. At this point, the blocks should measure 12½-inches square.

MAKE 4

Step 2

Sew a Step 1 block to both sides of the 2½ x 12½-inch Green #2 lattice strips, and press.

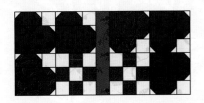

MAKE 2 BLOCK ROWS

Step 3

Referring to the quilt diagram, sew a Step 2 block row to both sides of a 2½ x 26½-inch Green #2 lattice strip, and press.

Step 4

Sew the remaining 2½ x 26½-inch Green #2 strips to the top and bottom of the quilt center, and press.

Step 5

Attach the 2½ x 30½-inch Green #2 side inner border strips to the quilt center, and press.

BORDER

Note: The yardage given allows for the border strips to be cut on the crosswise grain.

Red Plaid fabric:
Cut four 5½ x 30½-inch strips for the outer border.

Green Print #3 fabric:
Cut four 5½-inch corner squares.

ATTACHING THE BORDER

Step 1

Attach the top and bottom Red Plaid borders to the quilt, and press.

Step 2

Sew the Green corner squares to both ends of the remaining border strips, and

press. Sew the borders to the sides of the quilt, and press.

PUTTING IT ALL TOGETHER

Step 1

Trim the backing fabric and batting so they are 4-inches larger than the quilt top dimensions.

Step 2

Mark quilting designs on the quilt top. Layer the backing, batting, and quilt top, and quilt as desired. When quilting is complete, hand baste the three layers together a scant ¼-inch from the quilt top edge. Trim excess batting and backing even with the quilt top.

BINDING

From the binding fabric:

Cut five 2¼ x 42-inch strips.

Sew the binding to the quilt using ¼-inch seam allowance. This measurement will produce a ³⁄₈-inch finished double binding.

BINDING AND DIAGONAL PIECING

See General Instructions on page 140.

Little Red  House

58 x 72-inches

FABRICS AND SUPPLIES

- Yardage is based on 42-inch wide fabric.

- 1⅛ yards Red Plaid for houses

- ½ yard Green Print #1 for roofs

- ⅞ yard Black Print for doors, windows, chimneys, lattice posts, and inner border

- ⅓ yard Gold Print for pieced section at the base of the house

- ⅓ yard Green Print #2 for pieced section at the base of the house

- ¾ yard Beige Print for background

- ⅝ yard Green Print #3 for lattice strips

- 1⅞ yards Red Print for outer border

- ⅔ yard Binding fabric

- 3½ yards Backing fabric

- Quilt batting, at least 62 x 76 inches

- Rotary cutter, mat, and wide, clear-plastic ruler with ⅛-inch markings are necessary tools in attaining accuracy. A 6 x 24-inch ruler is recommended.

HOUSE BLOCKS
Make 12

Red Plaid fabric:

Cut three 4½ x 42-inch strips. From these strips cut twelve 4½ x 8½-inch rectangles.

Cut three 3½ x 42-inch strips. From these strips cut twenty four 3½ x 4½-inch rectangles.

FABRIC KEY

Red Plaid

Green Print #1

Green Print #2

Green Print #3

Beige Print

Black Print

Gold Print

Red Print

Cut three 1½ x 42-inch strips. From these strips cut twenty four 1½ x 4½-inch rectangles.

Cut three 1½ x 42-inch strips. From these strips cut thirty six 1½ x 2½-inch rectangles.

Green Print #1 fabric:
Cut three 4½ x 42-inch strips. From these strips cut twenty four 4½-inch squares.

Black Print fabric:
Cut two 2 x 42-inch strips. From these strips cut twelve 2 x 6½-inch rectangles.

Cut two 2½ x 42-inch strips. From these strips cut twelve 2½ x 3½-inch rectangles and twelve 2½-inch squares.

Gold Print fabric:
Cut five 1½-inch strips. From these strips cut seventy two 1½ x 2½-inch rectangles.

Green #2 fabric:
Cut five 1½ x 42-inch strips. From these strips cut seventy two 1½ x 2½-inch rectangles.

Beige Print fabric:
Cut two 4½ x 42-inch strips. From these strips cut twelve 4½-inch squares.

Cut two 3 x 42-inch strips. From these strips cut twelve 3 x 6½-inch rectangles.

Cut three 2½ x 42-inch strips. From these strips cut twelve 2½ x 8½-inch rectangles.

PIECING

Step 1

Position the 4½-inch Beige square at the left corner of the 4½ x 8½-inch Red rectangle. Draw a diagonal line on the Beige square and stitch on the line. Trim the seam allowance to ¼-inch, and press. Position a 4½-inch Green #1 square on the opposite corner of the Red rectangle. Draw a diagonal line on the Green square, and stitch, trim, and press. Sew the 2½ x 8½-inch Beige rectangle to the top of this unit, and press.

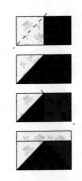

MAKE 12

Step 2

Sew together the 2 x 6½-inch Black rectangle and the 3 x 6½-inch Beige rectangle, and press. Position a 4½-inch Green #1 square at the lower edge of this unit. Draw a diagonal line on the Green square and stitch on the line. Trim the seam allowance to ¼-inch, and press.

MAKE 12

Step 3

Sew together the units from Step 1 and Step 2, and press.

MAKE 12

Step 4

Sew the 1½ x 2½-inch Red rectangle to the top of the 2½ x 3½-inch Black rectangle, and press. Sew the remaining 1½ x 2½-inch Red rectangles to the top and bottom of the 2½-inch Black squares, and press.

DOOR   WINDOW

MAKE 12

Step 5

Sew the $3^{1}/_{2}$ x $4^{1}/_{2}$-inch Red rectangles to both sides of the door unit, and press. Sew the $1^{1}/_{2}$ x $4^{1}/_{2}$-inch Red rectangles to both sides of the window unit, and press. Sew these units together, and press.

MAKE 12

Step 6

Sew together six each of the $1^{1}/_{2}$ x $2^{1}/_{2}$-inch Green #2 and Gold rectangles, and press.

MAKE 12

Step 7

Sew together the units from Step 3, Step 5, and Step 6, and press.

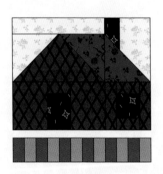

MAKE 12

LATTICE AND BORDERS

Note: The yardage given allows for the lattice and border strips to be cut on the crosswise grain. Diagonally piece the strips as needed.

Black Print fabric:

Cut six $2^{1}/_{2}$ x 42-inch strips. From these strips cut six $2^{1}/_{2}$-inch lattice posts. The remaining strips will be used for the inner border strips.

Green Print #3 fabric:

Cut six $2^{1}/_{2}$ x 42-inch strips. From these strips cut seventeen $2^{1}/_{2}$ x $12^{1}/_{2}$-inch lattice strips.

Red Print fabric:

Cut seven $7^{1}/_{2}$ x 42-inch strips for the outer border.

QUILT ASSEMBLY
Step 1

Sew together three house blocks and two $2^{1}/_{2}$ x $12^{1}/_{2}$-inch Green #3 lattice strips, and press.

MAKE 4 BLOCK ROWS

Step 2

Sew together three $2^{1}/_{2}$ x $12^{1}/_{2}$-inch Green #3 lattice strips and two $2^{1}/_{2}$-inch Black lattice posts, and press.

MAKE 3 LATTICE STRIPS

Step 3

Sew together the Step 1 block rows and the Step 2 lattice strips, and press.

Attaching the Borders

Step 1

Measure the quilt from left to right through the center. Cut two 2½-inch wide Black inner border strips to this measurement. Sew to the top and bottom of the quilt, and press.

Step 2

Measure the quilt from top to bottom through the center. Cut two 2½-inch wide Black inner border strips to this measurement. Sew to the sides of the quilt, and press.

Step 3

Measure the quilt from left to right through the center. Cut two 7½-inch wide Red outer border strips to this measurement. Sew to the top and bottom of the quilt, and press.

Step 4

Measure the quilt from top to bottom through the center. Cut two 7½-inch wide Red outer border strips to this measurement. Sew to the sides of the quilt, and press.

Putting it All Together

Step 1

Cut the 3½ yard length of backing fabric in half crosswise to make two 1¾ yard lengths. Sew the two lengths together along the long edge. Trim the backing fabric and batting so they are 4-inches larger than the quilt top dimensions.

Step 2

Mark quilting designs on the quilt top. Layer the backing, batting, and quilt top, and quilt as desired. When quilting is complete, hand baste the three layers together a scant ¼-inch from the quilt top edge. Trim excess batting and backing even with the quilt top.

Binding

From the binding fabric:

Cut seven 2¾ x 42-inch strips.

Sew the binding to the quilt using a ⅜-inch seam allowance. This measurement will produce a ½-inch wide finished double binding.

Binding and Diagonal Piecing

See General Instructions on page 140.

Reach for the Sun
Table Runner

Sue Smith

...ches

...AND SUPPLIES
...ased on 42-inch

...Print for

...Print for

...Print for

...t for

...for

...ic

...20 x 56-inches.

- Rotary cutter, mat, and wide clear-plastic ruler with ⅛-inch markings are necessary tools in attaining accuracy.

A 6 x 24-inch ruler is recommended.

SUNFLOWER BLOCKS
Make 3

Black Print fabric:
Cut one 4½ x 42-inch strip. From this strip cut seven 4½-inch squares.

Gold Print fabric:
Cut four 2½ x 42-inch strips. From these strips cut fifty six 2½-inch squares. Set thirty two aside to be used in the border.

Cut one 1½-inch strip. From this strip cut twenty eight 1½-inch squares.

Brown Print fabric:
Cut three 2½ x 42-inch strips. From these strips cut thirty six 2½-inch squares.

Cut two 2½ x 42-inch strips. From these strips cut twelve 2½ x 4½-inch rectangles.

Good buys can be found for old unmarked crocks and jars, especially when the cover is missing. They still make great display pieces, as well as flower pots. When using water with fresh flowers, insert a glass jar within the pot. Sometimes the very old pots have cracks—and will leak.

Purchase interesting dishes— even if they are just a partial set. Sometimes plates alone add a lot of character to a table or cupboard.

FABRIC KEY

Gold Print

Black Print

Brown Print

Beige Print

Green Print

Beige Print fabric:

Cut three 2½ x 42-inch strips. From these strips cut twenty four 2½ x 4½-inch rectangles.

Cut one 2½ x 42-inch strip. From this strip cut twelve 2½-inch squares.

PIECING

Step 1

Position 1½-inch Gold squares on the corners of a 4½-inch Black square. Draw a diagonal line on the Gold squares and stitch on the line. Trim the seam allowances to ¼-inch, and press.

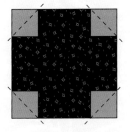

MAKE 7 FLOWER CENTERS

Set four aside to be used in the border.

Step 2

Position a 2½-inch Brown square on the corner of a 2½ x 4½-inch Beige rectangle. Draw a diagonal line on

the Brown square and stitch on the line. Trim the seam allowance to ¼-inch, and press. Repeat this process at the opposite corner of the Beige rectangle.

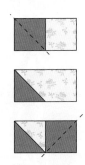

MAKE 12

Step 3

Sew 2½ x 4½-inch Beige rectangles to both sides of a Step 2 unit, and press.

MAKE 6

Step 4

Position a 2½-inch Gold square on the corner of a 2½ x 4½-inch Brown rectangle. Draw a diagonal line on the Gold square and stitch on the line. Trim the seam allowances to ¼-inch, and press.

Repeat this process at the opposite corner of the Brown rectangle.

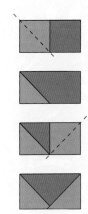

MAKE 12

Step 5

Sew 2½-inch Brown squares to both sides of a Step 4 unit, and press. Sew 2½-inch Beige squares to both sides of this unit, and press.

MAKE 6

Step 6

Sew Step 4 units to both sides of the Step 1 flower center. Sew Step 2 units to both sides of this unit, and press.

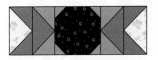

MAKE 3

Step 7

Sew together the units from Steps 3, 5 and 6, and press. At this point the blocks should measure 12½-inches square.

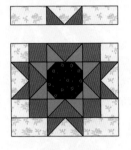

MAKE 3

BORDER AND LATTICE

Note: The yardage given allows for the lattice and border strips to be cut on the crosswise grain.

Green Print fabric:

Cut two 4½ x 40½-inch strips.

Cut two 2½ x 40½-inch strips.

Cut two 4½ x 12½-inch strips.

Cut four 2½ x 12½-inch strips.

Cut eight 2½ x 4½-inch rectangles.

Cut four 2½ -inch squares.

Gold Print fabric:

The thirty two 2½ -inch squares were cut in the Sunflower block section page 77.

ATTACHING THE LATTICE AND BORDERS

Step 1

Referring to the quilt diagram, sew together the three sunflower blocks and two 2½ x 12½-inch Green lattice strips, and press.

Step 2

Referring to the diagram, position 2½-inch Gold squares on opposite corners of a 4½ x 12½-inch Green strip. Draw diagonal lines on the Gold squares and stitch on the lines. Trim the seam allowances to ¼-inch, and press. Repeat this process for the remaining corners of the Green strip. Add a 2½ x 12½-inch Green strip to this unit.

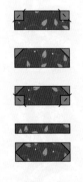

MAKE 2

Step 3

Sew the Step 2 border strips to the short ends of the quilt center, and press.

Step 4

Position 2½-inch Gold squares on opposite corners of a 4½ x 40½-inch Green strip. Draw diagonal lines on the Gold squares, stitch on the line, and trim the seam allowance to ¼-inch. Repeat for the remaining corners and add a 2½ x 40½-inch Green strip to this unit, and press.

MAKE 2

Step 5

Position a 2½-inch Gold square on the corner of a 2½ x 4½-inch Green rectangle. Draw a diagonal line on the Gold square and stitch on the line. Trim the seam allowance to ¼-inch, and press. Repeat this process at the opposite corner of the Green rectangle.

.

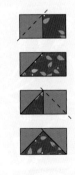

MAKE 8

Step 6

Referring to the diagram, sew a Step 5 unit to each flower center unit, and press. Sew a 2½-inch Green square to the remaining Step 5 units, and press. Sew these units together, and press.

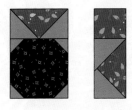

MAKE 4

Step 7

Sew the Step 6 units to both ends of the Step 4 border strips, and press. Sew the border strips to the long sides of the quilt center, and press.

MAKE 2

PUTTING IT ALL TOGETHER

Step 1

Trim the backing fabric and batting so they are 4-inches larger than the quilt top dimensions.

Step 2

Mark quilting designs on the quilt top. Layer the backing, batting, and quilt top, and quilt as desired. When quilting is complete, hand baste the three layers together a scant ¼-inch from the quilt top edge. Trim excess batting and backing even with the quilt top.

BINDING

From the binding fabric:

Cut four 2¼ x 42-inch strips.

Sew the binding to the quilt using a ¼-inch seam allowance. This measurement will produce a ³⁄₈-inch wide finished double binding.

BINDING AND DIAGONAL PIECING

See General Instructions on page 140.

A Welcoming Touch...

Use quilts as tablecloths and small wall quilts as table runners when tables are not actively being used for meal service. They add an amazing amount of color and visual warmth.

Hearts in the Corner

17-inches square

FABRICS AND SUPPLIES
Yardage is based on 42-inch wide fabric.

- $1/4$ yard Red Print for hearts and fifth border

- $1/3$ yard Beige Print for background, first and third borders

- $1/3$ yard Green Print for triangle blocks, Nine-Patch block, second border and fourth border

- $1/4$ yard Binding fabric

- $5/8$ yard Backing fabric

- Quilt batting, at least 21-inches square

- A rotary cutter, mat, and wide clear-plastic ruler with $1/8$-inch markings are necessary tools in attaining accuracy. A 6 x 24-inch ruler is recommended.

HEART BLOCKS
Make 4

Red Print fabric:
Cut four $2^{1}/_{2}$ x $3^{1}/_{2}$-inch rectangles.
Cut four $1^{1}/_{2}$ x $2^{1}/_{2}$-inch rectangles.

Beige Print fabric:
Cut four $1^{1}/_{2}$-inch squares.
Cut sixteen 1-inch squares.

PIECING
Step 1
Position 1-inch Beige squares on the upper corners of a $1^{1}/_{2}$ x $2^{1}/_{2}$-inch Red rectangle. Draw a diagonal line on the Beige squares, and stitch on the lines. Trim the seam allowances to $1/4$-inch, and press. Sew a $1^{1}/_{2}$-inch Beige square to the right hand side of this unit, trim, and press.

Make this small project for a Valentine's Day tea or as a gift for a special friend.

The flowers have simply been air dried by hanging them upside down in a dry area, away from direct sunlight. It is a fun way to preserve a special bouquet. These roses were brought to me along with a bottle of wine when our son-in-law asked for our daughter's hand in marriage. It was a wonderful, sweet, old-fashioned gesture, and these flowers bring back that special evening each time I look at them.

FABRIC KEY

Red Print

Beige Print

Green Print

MAKE 4

Step 2

Position 1-inch Beige squares on the upper corners of a $2^{1}/_{2}$ x $3^{1}/_{2}$-inch Red rectangle. Draw a diagonal line on the Beige squares, and stitch on the lines. Trim the seam allowances to $^{1}/_{4}$-inch, and press. Sew this unit to the Step 1 unit, and press.

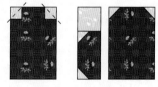

MAKE 4

TRIANGLE BLOCKS
Make 4

Beige Print and Green Print fabrics:

Cut two $4^{1}/_{4}$-inch squares.

PIECING
Step 1

Cut the squares diagonally into quarters, forming eight Beige triangles and eight Green triangles.

Step 2

Layer a Green triangle on a Beige triangle. Stitch along one of the bias edges, being careful not to stretch the triangles. Repeat for the remaining Beige and Green triangles. Make sure you sew with the Green triangle on top, and along the same bias edge of each triangle set, so that your pieced triangle units will all have the Green triangles on the same side, and press.

Step 3

Sew the Step 2 triangle units together in pairs to make the triangle blocks, and press. At this point the block should measure $3^{1}/_{2}$-inches square.

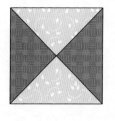

MAKE 4

NINE-PATCH BLOCK

Beige Print fabric:

Cut four $1^{1}/_{2}$-inch squares.

Green Print fabric:

Cut five $1^{1}/_{2}$-inch squares.

PIECING

Sew $1^{1}/_{2}$-inch Green squares to both sides of two Beige squares. Sew $1^{1}/_{2}$-inch Beige squares to both sides of a Green square. Press the seam allowances toward the darker fabric. Sew the units together.

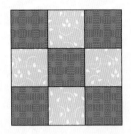

QUILT CENTER

Referring to the quilt diagram, sew the heart blocks, triangle blocks, and Nine-Patch block together in three horizontal rows, and press. Sew the rows together, and press.

BORDERS

Note: The yardage given allows for the border strips to be cut on the crosswise grain.

Beige Print fabric:

Cut one 1 x 42-inch strip for the first border.

Cut two 1½ x 42-inch strips for the third border.

Green Print fabric:

Cut three 1 x 42-inch strips for the second and fourth borders.

Red Print fabric:

Cut two 2 x 42-inch strips for the fifth border.

ATTACHING THE BORDERS

Step 1

Measure the quilt from left to right through the center. Cut two, 1-inch wide Beige border strips to this measurement. Sew the border strips to the top and bottom of the quilt, and press.

Step 2

Measure the quilt from top to bottom through the center. Cut two 1-inch wide Beige border strips to this measurement. Sew the border strips to the sides of the quilt, and press.

Step 3

To attach the 1-inch Green second border strips, refer to Steps 1 and 2.

Step 4

To attach the 1½-inch Beige third border strips, refer to Steps 1 and 2.

Step 5

To attach the 1-inch wide Green fourth border strips, refer to Steps 1 and 2.

Step 6

To attach the 2-inch wide Red fifth border strips, refer to Steps 1 and 2.

PUTTING IT ALL TOGETHER

Step 1

Trim the backing fabric and batting so they are 4-inches larger than the quilt top dimensions.

Step 2

Mark quilting designs on the quilt top. Layer the backing, batting, and quilt top, and quilt as desired. When quilting is complete, hand baste the three layers together a scant ¼-inch from the quilt top edge. Trim excess batting and backing even with the quilt top.

BINDING

From the binding fabric:

Cut two 2¼ x 42-inch strips. Sew the binding to the quilt using a ¼-inch seam allowance. This measurement will produce a ⅜-inch wide finished double binding.

BINDING AND DIAGONAL PIECING

See General Instructions on page 140.

Mini Christmas *Stocking*

11-inches long

FABRICS AND SUPPLIES

Yardage is based on 42-inch wide fabric.

- Twenty one 2½-inch squares Light to Medium Prints for stocking front

- Twenty one 2½-inch squares Dark Prints for stocking front

- 12 x 14-inch piece of Coordinating Fabric for stocking back

- ⅓ yard lining fabric

- ⅓ yard Black Print for facing and bias binding

- Two 12 x 14-inch pieces of quilt batting

- Pearl cotton for tying

- Rotary cutter, mat and wide clear-plastic ruler with ⅛-inch markings are necessary tools in attaining accuracy. A 6 x 24-inch ruler is recommended.

STOCKING UNIT

Step 1

Sew the 2½-inch Light to Medium squares and the Dark squares together in six rows of seven squares each, alternating the colors.

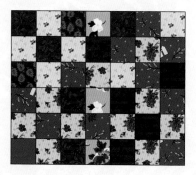

Step 2

Cut the lining fabric into two 12 x 14-inch pieces. Layer the lining, batting, and pieced stocking front. Using the pearl cotton, tie the layers together at the intersections of the squares.

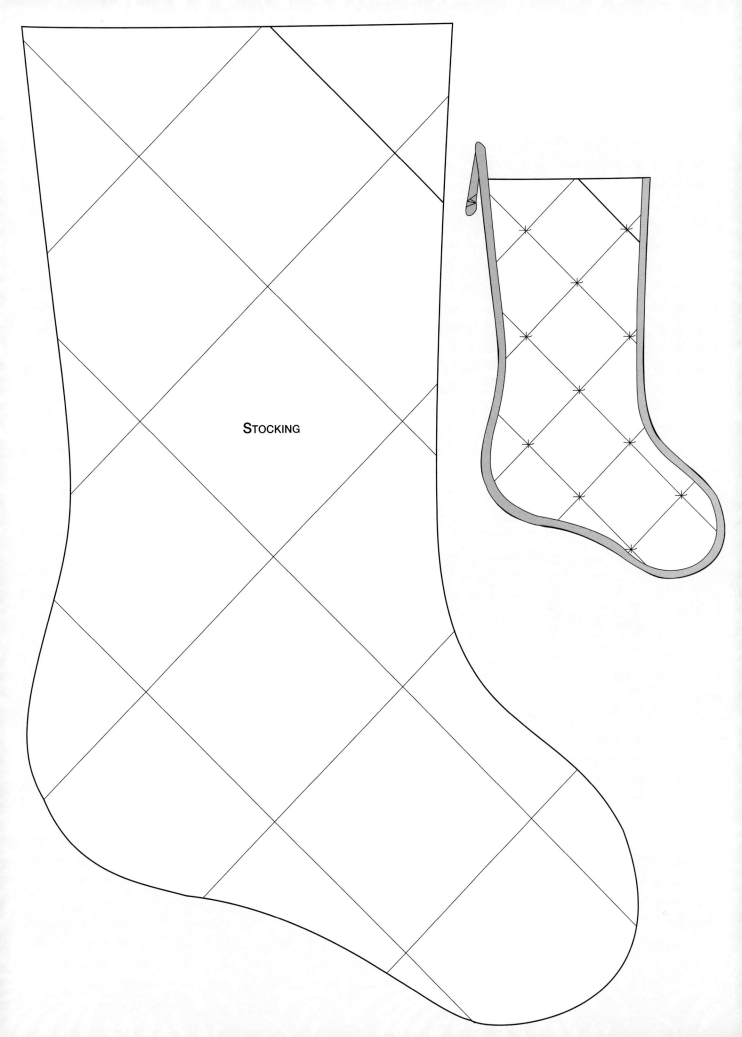

STOCKING

Step 3

Position the stocking pattern on the pieced front unit and cut out the stocking. Baste the edges together a scant $1/4$-inch from the edges.

Step 4

Layer and pin together the stocking back, batting, and lining fabric. Lay the stocking front unit on top of these layers, lining sides together. Trim the stocking back unit even with the stocking front. Remove the front unit from the back unit. Baste the back unit layers together.

Step 5

From the Black Print fabric, cut two $2^1/2$ x $6^1/2$-inch facing strips. Fold the strips in half lengthwise, wrong sides together, and press.

Step 6

With right sides together and raw edges even, stitch the facing to the stocking top edge with a $1/4$-inch seam allowance. Fold the facing to the inside of the stocking and hand stitch in place. Trim the ends even with the stocking.

Step 7

Repeat Step 6 for adding the facing to the stocking back.

Step 8

Layer the stocking front and back units, lining sides together. Stitch the six layers together with a $1/4$-inch seam allowance.

BINDING OUTER EDGES OF STOCKING

Black Print fabric:
Cut $2^1/2$-inch wide bias strips to make a strip 36-inches long.

ATTACHING THE BINDING

Step 1

Diagonally piece the Black bias strips together. Fold the binding strip in half lengthwise, wrong sides together, and press.

Step 2

Lay the binding on the stocking front, starting at the upper right side, with the raw edges even. Extend the binding $1/2$-inch beyond the top of the stocking. Stitch the binding to the stocking using a $1/4$-inch seam allowance, easing in extra binding at the heel and toe so they won't "cup."

Continue sewing the binding around the stocking.

Step 3

Fold under the $1/2$-inch extension and turn the folded edge of the binding to the back of the stocking. Hand stitch in place.

Step 4

To make the hanger, continue to sew the folded edges of the binding together. Tie a knot in the end, and stitch the tie to the stocking making a 3-inch hanger.

Harvest
Patchwork

The warmth of autumn's glorious colors create a cozy quilt and an inviting reading corner.

The table was formerly a drop-leaf kitchen table. Its legs were shortened and then the table was painted and stenciled to make a charming side table.

48-inches square

FABRICS AND SUPPLIES

Yardage is based on 42-inch wide fabric.

- $5/8$ yard Red Print for Blocks A and B

- $5/8$ yard Green Print for Block A

- $2/3$ yard Gold Print for Blocks A and B and corner squares

- $3/4$ yard Beige Print for background

- $3/8$ yard Black and Brown Print for inner border

- $2/3$ yard Green Floral for outer border

- $1/2$ yard Binding fabric

- 3 yards Backing fabric

- Quilt batting, at least 52-inches square

- Rotary cutter, mat, and wide clear-plastic ruler with $1/8$-inch markings are necessary tools in attaining accuracy. A 6 x 24-inch ruler is recommended.

BLOCK A
Make 5

Red Print fabric:
Cut four $2^{1}/_{2}$ x 42-inch strips. From these strips cut sixty $2^{1}/_{2}$-inch squares.

Green Print fabric:
Cut four $2^{1}/_{2}$ x 42-inch strips. From these strips cut sixty $2^{1}/_{2}$-inch squares.

Cut two $2^{7}/_{8}$ x 42-inch strips.

Beige Print fabric:
Cut five $2^{1}/_{2}$ x 42-inch strips. From these strips cut forty $2^{1}/_{2}$ x $4^{1}/_{2}$-inch rectangles.

Cut two $2^{7}/_{8}$ x 42-inch strips.

Fabric Key

Green Print

Beige Print

Gold Print

Green Floral

Red Print

Black and Brown Print

Gold Print fabric:

Cut five 4½-inch squares.

PIECING

Step 1

Layer the 2⅞ x 42-inch Green and Beige strips in pairs, and press. Cut the layered strips into twenty 2⅞-inch squares, taking care not to shift the layers as you cut.

CROSSCUT 20

Step 2

Cut the layered squares in half diagonally. Stitch ¼-inch from the diagonal edge of each pair of triangles, and press. At this point each triangle-pieced square should measure 2½-inches square.

MAKE 40

Step 3

Sew together 20 triangle-pieced squares and twenty 2½-inch Green squares in pairs, and press. Sew together 20 triangle-pieced squares and twenty 2½-inch Red squares in pairs, and press. Sew these twenty units together in pairs, and press.

MAKE 20

MAKE 20

MAKE 20

Step 4

Position a 2½-inch Green square at the corner of a 2½ x 4½-inch Beige rectangle. Draw a diagonal line on the Green square and stitch on the line. Trim the seam allowance to ¼-inch, and press. Repeat this process at the opposite corner of the Beige rectangle.

MAKE 20

Step 5

Position a 2½-inch Red square at the corner of a 2½ x 4½-inch Beige rectangle. Draw a diagonal line on the Red square and stitch on the line. Trim the seam to ¼-inch, and press. Repeat this process at the opposite corner of the Beige rectangle.

MAKE 20

Step 6

Sew the Step 4 and Step 5 units together in pairs, and press.

MAKE 20

Step 7

Sew Step 6 units to the top and bottom of the $4\frac{1}{2}$-inch Gold squares, and press.

MAKE 5

Step 8

Sew the Step 3 units to the top and bottom of the remaining Step 6 units, and press.

MAKE 10

Step 9

Sew the Step 8 units to both sides of the Step 7 units, and press. At this point the blocks should measure $12\frac{1}{2}$-inches square.

MAKE 5

BLOCK B

Make 4

Red Print fabric:

Cut one $5\frac{1}{4}$ x 42-inch strip. From this strip cut eight $5\frac{1}{4}$-inch squares. Cut the squares diagonally into quarters, forming 32 triangles.

Beige Print fabric:

Cut one $5\frac{1}{4}$ x 42-inch strip. From this strip cut eight $5\frac{1}{4}$-inch squares. Cut the squares diagonally into quarters, forming 32 triangles.

Gold Print fabric:

Cut three $4\frac{1}{2}$ x 42-inch strips. From these strips cut twenty $4\frac{1}{2}$-inch squares.

PIECING

Step 1

Layer a Red triangle on a Beige triangle. Stitch a $\frac{1}{4}$-inch seam along one of the bias edges, being careful not to stretch the triangles, and press. Repeat for the remaining triangles. Make sure you sew with the Red triangle on top, and along the same bias edge of each triangle set, so that your pieced triangle units will all have the Red triangle on the same side.

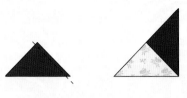

MAKE 32

Step 2

Sew the Step 1 triangle units together in pairs to make the triangle blocks, and press. At this point, the blocks should measure 4½-inches square.

MAKE 16

Step 3

Sew the Step 2 triangle blocks to the top and bottom of the 4½-inch Gold squares, and press. Make a total of 4 of these units.

Step 4

Sew the 4½-inch Gold squares to the top and bottom of the remaining Step 2 triangle blocks, and press. Make a total of 8 of these units.

Step 5

Sew the Step 4 units to both sides of the Step 3 units, and press. At this point the blocks should measure 12½-inches square.

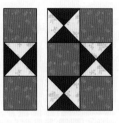

MAKE 4

Step 6

Referring to the quilt diagram, sew the A and B blocks together in rows, and press. Sew the rows together, and press.

BORDERS

Note: The yardage given allows for the border strips to be cut on the crosswise grain.

Black and Brown Print fabric:
Cut four 2½ x 42-inch strips for the inner border.

Green Floral fabric:
Cut four 4½ x 42-inch strips for the outer border.

Gold Print fabric:
Cut four 4½-inch corner squares.

ATTACHING THE BORDERS
Step 1

Measure the quilt from left to right through the center, and cut two 2½-inch wide Black and Brown Print borders to this length. Sew to the top and bottom of the quilt, and press.

Step 2

Measure the quilt from top to bottom through the center, and cut two 2½-inch wide Black and Brown Print borders to this length. Sew to the sides of the quilt, and press.

Step 3

Measure the quilt from left to right through the center, and cut two 4½-inch wide Green Floral borders to this length. Sew to the top and bottom of the quilt, and press.

Step 4

Measure the quilt from top to bottom including seam allowances, but not the borders just added. Cut two,

$4^{1}/_{2}$-inch wide Green Floral borders to this measurement. Add the $4^{1}/_{2}$-inch Gold corner squares to the ends of these strips, and press. Sew to the sides of the quilt, and press.

PUTTING IT ALL TOGETHER

Step 1

Cut the three yard length of backing in half crosswise to make two $1^{1}/_{2}$ yard lengths. Sew the two lengths together along the long edge. Trim the backing fabric and batting so they are 4-inches larger than the quilt top dimensions.

Step 2

Mark quilting designs on the quilt top. Layer the backing, batting and quilt top, and quilt as desired. When quilting is complete, hand baste the three layers together a scant $1/_{4}$-inch from the quilt top edge. Trim excess batting and backing even with the quilt top.

BINDING

From the binding fabric:

Cut five $2^{3}/_{4}$ x 42-inch strips. Sew the binding to the quilt using a $3/_{8}$-inch seam allowance. This measurement will produce a $1/_{2}$-inch wide finished double binding.

BINDING AND DIAGONAL PIECING

See General Instructions on page 140.

Lost *Mittens*

54 x 66-inches

FABRICS AND SUPPLIES

Yardage is based on 42-inch wide fabric.

- 7/8 yard Brown Plaid for appliqué foundation blocks

- 2 yards Green Floral for alternate blocks and outer border

- 3/4 yard Solid Green for side and corner triangles

- 1/2 yard Solid Black for inner border

- 1/4 yard each of Solid Red, Black, and Gold wool for mitten, star, and heart appliqués

- 1 1/4 yards Binding fabric

- 3 1/4 yards Backing fabric

- Quilt batting, at least 58 x 70-inches

- Template material for appliqués

- #8 Black and Gold pearl cotton thread

- Rotary cutter, mat, and wide clear-plastic ruler with 1/8-inch markings are necessary in attaining accuracy. A 6 x 24-inch ruler is recommended.

QUILT TOP

Brown Plaid fabric:
Cut three 9 x 42-inch strips. From these strips, cut twelve 9-inch squares.

Green Floral fabric:
Cut two 9 x 42-inch strips. From these strips cut six 9-inch squares.

Solid Green fabric:
Cut two 8-inch squares. Cut the squares in half diagonally for corner triangles.

Cut three 14-inch squares.

Cuddle up by a fire with this cozy quilt, some popcorn and good music. Appliquéd mittens of wool or flannel remind us of childhood romps in the snow and the oh-so-many lost mittens. Simple throw pillows covered in flannel are everyone's favorite and along with a quilt, create a very inviting room.

FABRIC KEY

Brown Plaid

Green Floral

Solid Green

Solid Black

Solid Red

Solid Gold

Cut the squares diagonally into quarters. You will be using only 10 of the 12 triangles for side triangles.

APPLIQUÉ
Step 1
Make templates for the mitten, heart, and star shapes. Trace the shapes onto the wool pieces, referring to the pattern pieces for color and quantities of each.

Step 2
Position the mittens on the Brown Plaid squares. With one strand of pearl cotton, buttonhole stitch around the mittens and stem stitch the cuff detail. Use black pearl cotton on the Gold and Red fabrics, and gold pearl cotton on the Black fabric. Using the buttonhole stitch, appliqué the hearts and stars to the mittens.

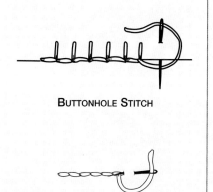

BUTTONHOLE STITCH

STEM STITCH

QUILT ASSEMBLY
Step 1
Lay out the mitten blocks, alternate blocks, and the side triangles, referring to the quilt diagram. Sew the blocks and triangles together in diagonal rows, and press.

Step 2
Sew the diagonal rows together, and press. Sew the corner triangles to the quilt center, and press.

Step 3
Using the rotary cutter, mat, and wide clear-plastic ruler, trim away the excess fabric from the side and corner triangles, making sure to allow 1/4-inch seam allowances beyond the block corners.

Refer to Trimming Side and Corner Triangles on page 142 for complete instructions.

BORDERS
Note: The yardage given allows for the border strips to be cut on the crosswise grain. Diagonally piece the strips as needed.

Solid Black fabric:
Cut five 2 1/2 x 42-inch strips for the inner border.

Green Floral fabric:
Cut six 8 x 42-inch strips for the outer border.

ATTACHING THE BORDERS
Step 1
Measure the quilt from left to right through the center. Cut two 2 1/2-inch wide Black inner border strips to this measurement. Sew the strips to the top and bottom of the quilt, and press. Measure the quilt from the top to the bottom through the center. Cut two 2 1/2-inch wide Black inner border strips to this measurement. Sew the strips to the sides of the quilt, and press.

Step 2
Measure the quilt from left to right through the center. Cut two 8-inch wide Green Floral outer border strips to this measurement. Sew the strips to the top and bottom of the quilt, and press. Measure the quilt from top to bottom through the center. Cut two 8-inch wide Green Floral outer border strips to this measurement. Sew the strips to the sides of the quilt, and press.

Putting it All Together

Step 1

Cut the $3\frac{1}{4}$ yard length of backing in half crosswise to make two $1\frac{5}{8}$-yard lengths. Sew the two lengths together along the long edge. Trim the backing fabric and batting so they are 4-inches larger than the quilt top dimensions.

Step 2

Mark quilting designs on the quilt top. Layer the backing, batting, and quilt top, and quilt as desired. When quilting is complete, hand baste the three layers together a scant $\frac{1}{4}$-inch from the quilt top edge. Trim excess batting and backing even with the quilt top.

Bias Binding

From the binding fabric:

Cut enough $6\frac{1}{2}$-inch wide bias strips to make a strip 260-inches long.

Sew the binding to the quilt using a 1-inch seam allowance. This measurement will produce a 1-inch wide finished double binding.

Binding and Diagonal Piecing

See General Instructions on page 140.

HEART

From the Solid Red and Gold
Trace 8 of each

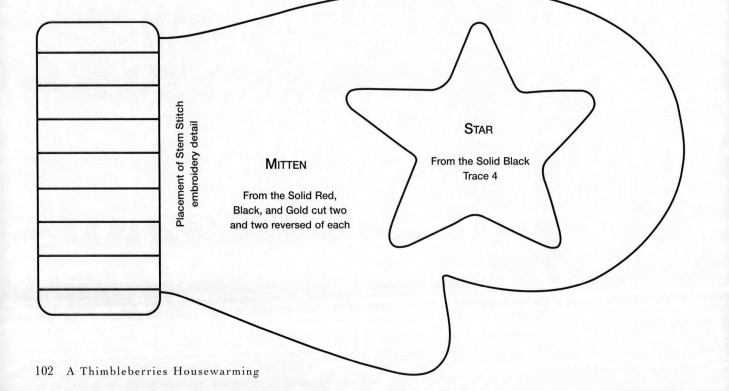

Placement of Stem Stitch
embroidery detail

MITTEN

From the Solid Red,
Black, and Gold cut two
and two reversed of each

STAR

From the Solid Black
Trace 4

North Pole *Plaid*

Curl up with a good book and this great flannel quilt. A simple, meandering quilting design is always appropriate for an all-over design and so practical for flannel quilts.

Meandering retains the softness and loft that makes flannel quilts so special. This quilt will become the family favorite.

70 x 90-inches

FABRICS AND SUPPLIES

Yardage is based on 42-inch wide fabric.

- 1⅝ yards Beige Floral fabric for block center

- 1¾ yards Green Print fabric for block strips

- 1 yard Gold Print fabric for block squares

- 2⅜ yards Red Print fabric for block strips

- 1 yard Binding fabric (bias cut)

- 5½ yards Backing fabric

- Quilt batting, at least 74 x 94-inches

- Rotary cutter, mat, and wide clear-plastic ruler with ⅛-inch markings are necessary tools in attaining accuracy. A 6 x 24-inch ruler is recommended.

PIECED BLOCKS
Make 63

Beige Floral fabric:
Cut nine 5½ x 42-inch strips for Strip Set A.

Green Print fabric:
Cut nine 3 x 42-inch strips for Strip Set A.

Cut five 5½ x 42-inch strips for Strip Set B.

Gold Print fabric:
Cut five 3 x 42-inch strips for Strip Set B.

Cut five 3 x 42-inch strips for Strip Set C.

Red Print fabric:
Cut five 8 x 42-inch strips for Strip Set C.

Cut thirteen 3 x 42-inch strips. From these strips cut sixty three 3 x 8-inch rectangles.

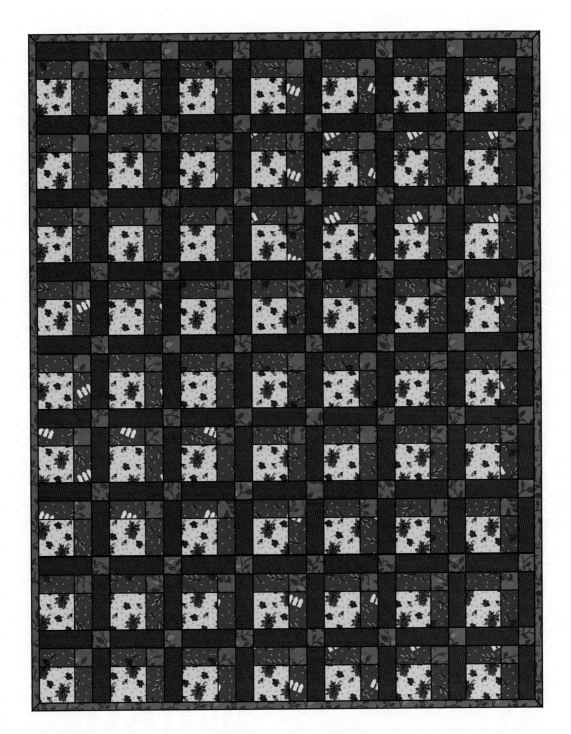

FABRIC KEY

Beige Floral

Green Print

Gold Print

Red Print

PIECING

Note: The blocks are made up of three strip sets. To minimize cutting and piecing, the fabrics are first cut into strips. These strips are then sewn together and cut into segments for the block assembly.

Step 1

To make Strip Set A, sew a $5\frac{1}{2}$ x 42-inch Beige Floral strip and a 3 x 42-inch Green strip together along the long edge, and press. Make nine Strip Set As and crosscut them into sixty three $5\frac{1}{2}$-inch wide segments.

$5\frac{1}{2}$" STRIP SET A

MAKE 9

Step 2

To make Strip Set B, sew a $5\frac{1}{2}$ x 42-inch Green strip and a 3 x 42-inch Gold strip together along the long edge, and press. Make five Strip Set Bs and crosscut them into sixty three, 3-inch wide segments.

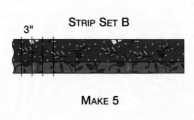

3" STRIP SET B

MAKE 5

Step 3

To make Strip Set C, sew an 8 x 42-inch Red Print strip and a 3 x 42-inch Gold Print strip together along the long edge, and press. Make five Strip Set Cs and crosscut them into sixty three 3-inch wide segments.

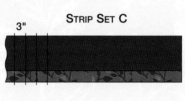

3" STRIP SET C

MAKE 5

Step 4

For each block you will need a Strip Set A, B, C, and one 3 x 8-inch Red Print rectangle.

Step 5

Refer to diagrams for strip set placement. Sew the strip sets and the 3 x 8-inch Red Print rectangle together. At this point the block should measure $10\frac{1}{2}$-inches square.

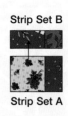
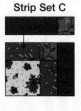

Strip Set B

Strip Set C

Strip Set A

MAKE 63 BLOCKS

Step 6

To assemble the quilt top, use the quilt diagram as a guide for block placement. Sew the blocks together in nine horizontal rows of seven blocks each. Press the seam allowances in alternating directions by rows so the seams will fit snugly together with less bulk. Sew the horizontal rows together matching the block intersections.

PUTTING IT ALL TOGETHER

Step 1

Cut the $5\frac{1}{2}$-yard length of backing in half crosswise to make two $2\frac{3}{4}$-yards lengths. Sew the two lengths together along the long edge. Trim the backing and batting so they are 4-inches larger than the quilt top dimensions.

Step 2

Mark quilting designs on the quilt top. Layer the backing, batting, and quilt top, and quilt as desired. When quilting is complete, hand baste the three layers together a scant $\frac{1}{4}$-inch from the quilt top edge. This basting prevents the layers from shifting when the binding is applied.

Bias Binding

From the binding fabric:

Cut enough $2\frac{3}{4}$-inch wide bias strips to make a strip approximately 340-inches long. Sew the binding on using a $\frac{3}{8}$-inch seam allowance. This measurement will produce a $\frac{1}{2}$-inch wide finished double binding.

See General Instructions on page 140.

A Welcoming Touch...

Stack quilts in a large basket or perhaps hang quilts on the rungs of a ladder to have handy for all to cuddle.

Fill cupboards and shelves with quilts using the mix of colors and patterns as artwork. To make a few quilts look like more quilts, fold them in an accordion fashion creating many folds of color.

April Showers

71³/₄-inches square

FABRICS AND SUPPLIES

Yardage is based on 42-inch wide fabric.

- 3¹/₄ yards Blue Print for Nine-Patch blocks, border, and tabs

- 1¹/₄ yards Tan Print for Nine-Patch blocks

- 3 yards Tan and Blue Plaid for alternate blocks, side and corner triangles, and bias binding

- 4¹/₂ yards Backing fabric

- Lightweight quilt batting, at least 76-inches square

- Twelve 1¹/₂-inch diameter ceramic star buttons

- Rotary cutter, mat, and wide clear-plastic ruler with ¹/₈-inch markings are necessary tools in attaining accuracy. A 6 x 24-inch ruler is recommended.

NINE-PATCH BLOCKS

Make 25

Blue Print fabric:
Cut thirteen 3¹/₂ x 42-inch strips.

Tan Print fabric:
Cut eleven 3¹/₂ x 42-inch strips.

PIECING

Step 1

Sew 3¹/₂ x 42-inch Blue strips to both sides of five 3¹/₂ x 42-inch Tan strips, and press. Cut the strip sets into segments.

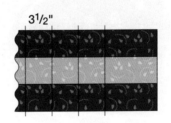

3¹/₂"

CROSSCUT 50

Bring a mixture of color and texture into the bath with a quilted shower curtain.

Use thin batting or prewashed flannel—90" wide is best.

Use tabs at the top—decorate with antique or pottery buttons.

A plant-stand table which holds and enamel pail, serves as a unique towel caddy.

FABRIC KEY

Blue Print

Tan Print

Tan and Blue Plaid

Step 2

Sew 3½ x 42-inch Tan strips to both sides of three 3½ x 42-inch Blue strips, and press. Cut the strip sets into segments.

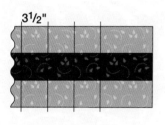

CROSSCUT 25

Step 3

Sew the Step 1 segments to both sides of the Step 2 segments, and press. At this point the Nine-Patch blocks should measure 9½-inches square.

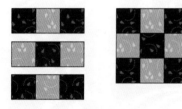

MAKE 25

QUILT CENTER

Tan and Blue Plaid fabric:

Cut four 9½ x 42-inch strips. From these strips cut sixteen 9½-inch squares for the alternate blocks.

Cut two 14½ x 42-inch strips. From these strips cut four 14½-inch squares. Cut these squares diagonally into quarters for a total of 16 side triangles. Also from these strips cut two 9-inch squares. Cut these squares in half diagonally for a total of 4 corner triangles.

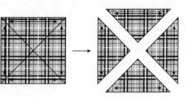

MAKE 16 SIDE TRIANGLES

Note: The side and corner triangles are larger than necessary and will be trimmed before the border is added.

ASSEMBLY
Step 1

Referring to the quilt diagram, sew the Nine-Patch blocks, the alternate blocks, and the side triangles together in diagonal rows. Press the seam allowances in alternating directions by rows so the seams will fit snugly together with less bulk.

Step 2

Pin the rows at the block intersections, and sew the rows together. Press the seam allowances in one direction.

Step 3

Sew the corner triangles to the quilt, and press.

Step 4

Trim away the excess fabric from the side and corner triangles, taking care to allow a ¼-inch seam allowance beyond the corners of each block. Refer to Trimming the Side and Corner Triangles on page 142 for complete instructions.

BORDER

Note: The yardage given allows for the border strips to be cut on the crosswise grain. Diagonally piece the strips as needed.

Blue Print fabric:

Cut eight 4½ x 42-inch strips for the border.

Attaching the Border

Step 1

Measure the quilt from left to right through the center. Cut two 4½-inch wide Blue border strips to this measurement. Sew these border strips to the quilt, and press.

Step 2

Measure the quilt from top to bottom through the center, including the borders just added. Cut two 4½-inch wide Blue border strips to this length. Sew these borders to the quilt, and press.

Putting it All Together

Step 1

Cut the 4½-yard length of backing in half crosswise to make two 2¼-yard lengths. Sew the two lengths together along the long edge. Remember to cut off the selvage. Trim the backing fabric and batting so they are 4-inches larger than the quilt top dimensions.

Step 2

Mark quilting designs on the quilt top. Layer the quilt top with the batting and backing, and quilt as desired. When quilting is complete, hand baste the three layers together with a scant ¼-inch from the quilt top edge. Trim excess backing and batting even with the quilt top.

Tabs

Blue Print fabric:

Cut four 6½ x 42-inch strips. From these strips cut twelve 6½ x 11-inch rectangles.

Making the Tabs

Fold each 6½ x 11-inch Blue rectangle in half lengthwise, wrong sides together, and press. Unfold and bring the raw edges to meet at the center fold line, press and fold at the center fold line. Topstitch close to both folded edges. The tabs will be attached after the binding.

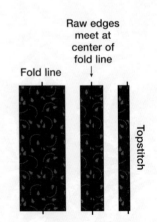

Raw edges meet at center of fold line

Fold line

Topstitch

MAKE 12

BIAS BINDING

Tan and Blue Plaid fabric:
Cut enough 2³/₄-inch wide bias strips to total 300-inches.

ATTACHING THE BINDING

Step 1

Sew the binding to both side edges of the shower curtain and to the bottom edge, using a ³/₈-inch seam allowance. This measurement will produce a ¹/₂-inch wide finished double binding. Leave the top edge unstitched.

Step 2

At the top edge of the shower curtain, mark twelve positions for the tabs.

Step 3

Fold each tab in half cross-wise, having raw edges even. Pin each tab in place on the front side of the shower curtain, having the raw edges of the curtain and tabs even. Pin in place.

Step 4

Continue to sew the binding to the top edge of the shower curtain.

Step 5

Turn the folded edge of the binding over the raw edges and to the back of the quilt so that the stitching lines do not show. Hand sew the binding in place, folding in the mitered corners as you stitch.

Step 6

Flip each tab up so only ⁵/₈-inch extends below the binding, and pin in place. Top stitch at both edges of each tab to secure it to the shower curtain. Sew a star ceramic button to each tab.

A Welcoming Touch...

The wide variety of beautiful towels now available is an inexpensive way to add glorious color to a bath. Stacked, piled, or bundled, the "splash" of color they add is the easiest answer to decorating a bathroom.

Unusual containers make ideal towel holders. Consider old enamel pails, fruit crates, wooden eggcrates, or large planters—all will add a decorative flair.

Fill an interesting vintage bowl, basket, or flowerpot with unwrapped bath soap bars. The scent is fresh and clean and, of course, it is nice to have soap always readily available.

Sawtooth Nine-Patch *Variation*

66 x 82-inches

FABRICS AND SUPPLIES
Yardage is based on 42-inch wide fabric.

- 2 yards Red Print for sawtooth, vertical strips, and corner squares

- 1¼ yards Brown and Black Print for Nine-Patch blocks and middle border

- 1½ yards Beige Print for background

- ¾ yard Red Check for alternate blocks

- ¾ yard Gold Print for inner border

- 1 yard Brown Floral for outer border

- ⅔ yard Binding fabric

- 4 yards Backing fabric

- Quilt batting, at least 70 x 86-inches

- Rotary cutter, mat, and wide clear-plastic ruler with ⅛-inch markings are necessary tools in attaining accuracy. A 6 x 24-inch ruler is recommended.

SAWTOOTH SECTIONS
Make 4

Red Print fabric:
Cut nine 2⅞ x 42-inch strips.

Cut seven 4½ x 42-inch strips. Diagonally piece the strips as needed and cut them into four 4½ x 66½-inch strips.

Beige Print fabric:
Cut nine 2⅞ x 42-inch strips.

PIECING
Step 1
Layer the 2⅞ x 42-inch Red and Beige strips in pairs, and press. Cut the layered strips into one-hundred thirty two 2⅞-inch squares.

A stack of like-sized trunks create wonderful visual storage and display.

Search for wooden tool caddies— they hold a variety of items, such as books, towels, extra quilts, and plants.

The color of old pine is especially complementary to quilts— old or new.

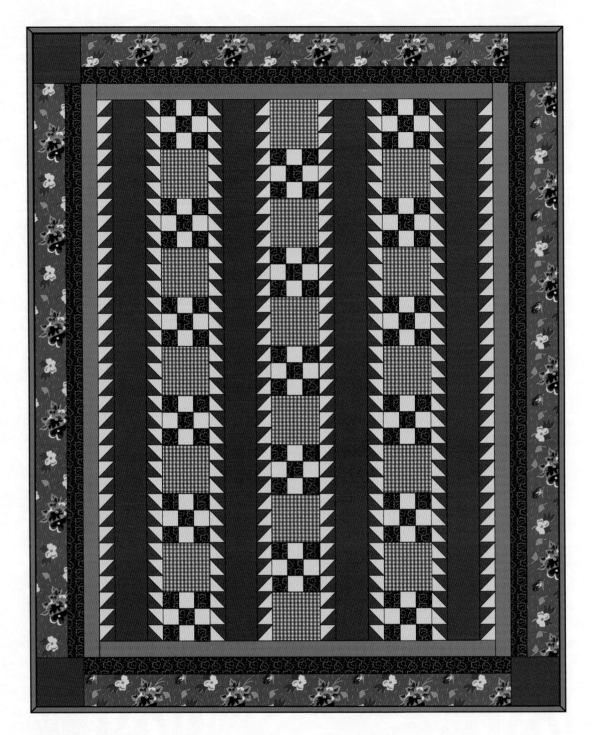

FABRIC KEY

Red Print

Brown and Black Print

Beige Print

Red Check

Gold Print

Brown Floral

Take care not to shift the layers as you cut.

2⁷/₈"

CROSSCUT 132

Step 2

Cut the layered squares in half diagonally. Stitch ¼-inch from the diagonal edge of each pair of triangles, and press. At this point each triangle-pieced square should measure 2½-inches square.

MAKE 264

Step 3

Sew together thirty three triangle-pieced squares, and press.

MAKE 4 STRIPS

For the reverse strips, sew together thirty three triangle-pieced squares, and press.

MAKE 4 STRIPS REVERSED

Step 4

Referring to the quilt diagram, sew the Step 3 sawtooth strips to both sides of the 4½ x 66½-inch Red vertical strips, and press.

NINE-PATCH BLOCKS
Make 17

Brown and Black Print fabric:

Cut eight 2½ x 42-inch strips.

Beige Print fabric:

Cut seven 2½ x 42-inch strips.

PIECING
Step 1

Sew 2½ x 42-inch Brown and Black strips to both sides of a 2½ x 42-inch Beige strip, and press. Make three strip sets. Cut the strip sets into segments.

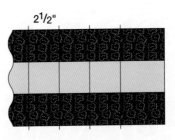

2½"

CROSSCUT 34

Step 2

Sew 2½ x 42-inch Beige strips to both sides of a 2½ x 42-inch Brown and Black strip, and press. Make two strip sets. Cut the strip sets into segments.

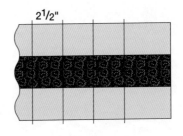

2½"

CROSSCUT 17

Step 3

Sew the Step 1 segments to both sides of the Step 2 segments, and press. At this point the Nine-Patch blocks should measure 6½-inches square.

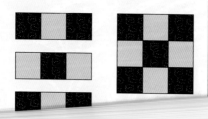

MAKE 17

QUILT CENTER

Red Check fabric:

Cut three 6½ x 42-inch strips. From these strips cut sixteen 6½-inch squares for the alternate blocks.

QUILT CENTER ASSEMBLY

Step 1

Referring to the quilt diagram, sew six Nine-Patch blocks and five 6½-inch Red Check alternate blocks together, and press. Make a total of two of these strips.

Step 2

Referring to the quilt diagram, sew five Nine-Patch blocks and six 6½-inch Red Check alternate blocks together, and press. Make only one strip.

Step 3

Referring to the quilt diagram, sew the sawtooth strips and the Step 1 and Step 2

BORDERS

Note: The yardage given allows for the border strips to be cut on the crosswise grain. Diagonally piece the strips as needed.

Gold Print fabric:

Cut seven 2½ x 42-inch strips for the inner border.

Brown and Black Print fabric:

Cut seven 2½ x 42-inch strips for the middle border.

Brown Floral fabric:

Cut seven 4½ x 42-inch strips for the outer border.

Red Print fabric:

Cut four 6½-inch corner squares.

ATTACHING THE BORDERS

Step 1

Measure the quilt from left

Cut the 2½-inch wide Gold border strips to this measurement. Sew to the top and bottom of the quilt, and press.

Step 2

Measure the quilt from top to bottom through the center. Cut the 2½-inch wide Gold border strips to this measurement. Sew to the sides of the quilt, and press.

Step 3

Sew the 2½-inch wide Brown and Black middle border strips to the 4½-inch wide Brown Floral outer border strips, and press.

Step 4

Measure the quilt from left to right through the center. Cut two 6½-inch wide Step 3 pieced border strips to this measurement. Sew the pieced border strips to the top and bottom of the quilt, and press.

Step 5

Measure the quilt from top to bottom including the seam allowances, but not the borders just added. Cut two $6^1/2$-inch wide Step 3 pieced border strips to this measurement. Add $6^1/2$-inch Red corner squares to the ends of these strips, and press. Sew the border strips to the sides of the quilt, and press.

PUTTING IT ALL TOGETHER

Step 1

Cut the 4 yard length of backing in half crosswise to make two 2-yard lengths. Sew the two lengths together along the long edge. Trim the backing fabric and batting so they are 4-inches larger than the quilt top dimensions.

Step 2

Mark quilting designs on the quilt top. Layer the backing, batting, and quilt top, and quilt as desired. When quilting is complete, hand baste the three layers together a scant $1/4$-inch from the quilt top edge. Trim excess batting and backing even with the quilt top.

BINDING

From the binding fabric:

Cut eight $2^3/4$ x 42-inch strips. Sew the binding to the quilt using a $3/8$-inch seam allowance. This measurement will produce a $1/2$-inch wide finished double binding.

BINDING AND DIAGONAL PIECING

See General Instructions on page 140.

A Welcoming Touch...

A quilt can be a bold, graphic statement in a contemporary setting, or charm its viewers with warmth in an intimate country setting.

Holiday Nine-*Patch*

96 x 109-inches

FABRICS AND SUPPLIES
Yardage is based on 42-inch wide fabric.

- 4½ yards Green Print for Nine-Patch blocks, inner border, and outer border

- 6½ yards Beige Print for alternate blocks, Nine-Patch blocks, and corner and side triangles

- 1 yard Red Print for narrow borders

- 1 yard Binding fabric

- 8¼ yards Backing fabric

- Quilt batting, at least 100 x 113-inches

- Rotary cutter, mat, and wide clear-plastic ruler with ⅛-inch markings are necessary tools in attaining accuracy. A 6 x 24-inch ruler is recommended.

NINE-PATCH BLOCKS
Make 210

Green Print fabric:
Cut thirty eight 1½ x 42-inch strips.

Beige Print fabric:
Cut thirty one 1½ x 42-inch strips.

PIECING
Step 1
Sew 1½ x 42-inch Green strips to both sides of fifteen 1½ x 42-inch Beige strips, and press. Make a total of fifteen strip sets. Cut the strip sets into segments.

1½"

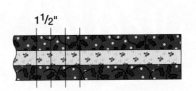

CROSSCUT 420

FABRIC KEY

Green Print

Beige Print

Red Print

Step 2

Sew $1\frac{1}{2}$ x 42-inch Beige strips to both sides of eight $1\frac{1}{2}$ x 42-inch Green strips, and press. Make a total of eight strip sets. Cut the strip sets into segments.

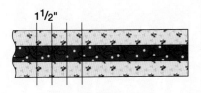

CROSSCUT 210

Step 3

Sew Step 1 segments to both sides of the Step 2 segments, and press. At this point the blocks should measure $3\frac{1}{2}$-inches square.

MAKE 210

LARGE NINE-PATCH BLOCKS
Make 42

Beige Print fabric:
Cut fifteen $3\frac{1}{2}$ x 42-inch strips. From these strips cut one-hundred sixty eight $3\frac{1}{2}$-inch squares.

PIECING
Step 1
Sew a Nine-Patch block to both sides of eighty four $3\frac{1}{2}$-inch Beige squares, and press.

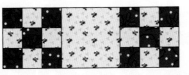

MAKE 84

Step 2
Sew $3\frac{1}{2}$-inch Beige squares to both sides of 42 Nine-Patch blocks, and press.

MAKE 42

Step 3

Sew the Step 1 units to both sides of the Step 2 units and press. At this point the blocks should measure $9\frac{1}{2}$-inches square.

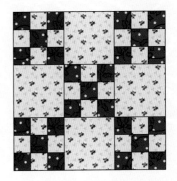

MAKE 42

QUILT CENTER
Beige Print fabric:
Cut eight $9\frac{1}{2}$ x 42-inch strips. From these strips cut thirty $9\frac{1}{2}$-inch squares for the alternate blocks.

Cut three 15 x 42-inch strips. From these strips cut six 15-inch squares. Cut the squares diagonally into quarters for a total of 24 triangles. You will be using 22 of them for the side triangles.

Cut two 8-inch squares. Cut the squares in half diagonally for a total of four corner triangles.

Quilt Center Assembly

Step 1

Referring to the quilt assembly diagram, sew the blocks and side triangles together in diagonal rows. Press the seam allowances toward the alternate blocks and the side triangles. Sew the diagonal rows together, and press. Sew the corner triangles to the quilt, and press.

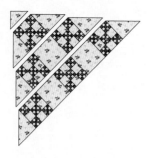

Assembly Diagram

Step 2

Trim the excess fabric from the side and corner triangles, making sure to allow a $1/4$-inch seam allowance beyond the corners of each block. Refer to Trimming Side and Corner Triangles on page 142 for complete instructions.

Red Print fabric:

Cut nineteen $1^1/2$ x 42-inch strips for the inner and middle borders.

Green Print fabric:

Cut ten $2^1/2$ x 42-inch strips for the inner border.

Cut eleven $6^1/2$ x 42-inch strips for the outer border.

Attaching the Borders

Step 1

Measure the quilt through the center from left to right. Cut two $1^1/2$-inch wide Red inner border strips to this measurement. Sew to the top and bottom of the quilt, and press.

Step 2

Measure the quilt through the center from top to bottom. Cut two $1^1/2$-inch wide Red inner border strips to this measurement. Sew to the sides of the quilt, and press.

this measurement. Sew to the top and bottom of the quilt, and press.

Step 4

Measure the quilt through the center from top to bottom. Cut two $2^1/2$-inch Green inner border strips to this measurement. Sew to the sides of the quilt, and press.

Step 5

Measure the quilt through the center from left to right. Cut two $1^1/2$-inch wide Red middle border strips to this measurement. Sew to the top and bottom of the quilt, and press.

Step 6

Measure the quilt through the center from top to bottom. Cut two $1^1/2$-inch wide Red middle border strips to this measurement. Sew to the sides of the quilt, and press.

Step 7

Measure the quilt through the center from left to right. Cut two $6^1/2$-inch wide

Green outer border strips to this measurement. Sew to the top and bottom of the quilt, and press.

Step 8

Measure the quilt through the center from top to bottom. Cut two 6½-inch wide Green outer border strips to this measurement. Sew to the sides of the quilt, and press.

PUTTING IT ALL TOGETHER

Step 1

Cut the 8¼ yard length of backing fabric in thirds crosswise to make three 2¾-yard lengths. Sew the three lengths together along the long edges. Trim the backing fabric and batting so they are 4-inches larger than the quilt top.

Step 2

Mark quilting designs on the quilt top. Layer the backing, batting and quilt top, and quilt as desired. When quilting is complete, hand baste the three layers together a scant ¼-inch from the quilt top edge. Trim excess batting and backing even with the quilt top.

BINDING

From the binding fabric:
Cut eleven 2¾ x 42-inch strips.

Sew the binding to the quilt using a ⅜-inch seam allowance. This measurement will produce a ½-inch wide finished double binding.

BINDING AND DIAGONAL PIECING

See General Instructions on page 140.

A Welcoming Touch...

To freshen stored bed linens, try adding 1 cup of white distilled vinegar to the rinse water of the wash cycle. Commercial fabric softeners also add a nice scent to bedding.

When making up the guestrooms consider dusting pillowcases and bed sheets with dusting powder. It is a luxurious welcome for the guest in your home.

Cherry Basket

94 x 111-inches

FABRICS AND SUPPLIES

Yardage is based on 42-inch wide fabric.

- $1/2$ yard Blue Floral for basket top triangles

- $1^7/8$ yards Green Print #1 for basket base and middle border

- $4^3/4$ yards Beige Print for basket and Nine-Patch background, and side and corner triangles

- $1^1/2$ yards Blue Print for basket handles, narrow borders, and corner squares

- $1^1/3$ yards Red Floral for Nine-Patch blocks

- $2^7/8$ yards Blue Plaid for outer border

- $1/4$ yard Red Print for cherry appliqués

- $5/8$ yard Green Print #2

for leaf and stem appliqués

- 1 yard Binding fabric

- $8^1/4$ yards Backing fabric

- 1 yard freezer paper for appliqué

- 5-inch square of lightweight cardboard for appliqués

- A manila folder for template

- Quilt batting, at least 98 x 115-inches

- Rotary cutter, mat, and wide clear-plastic ruler with $1/8$-inch markings are necessary tools in attaining accuracy. A 6 x 24-inch ruler is recommended.

BASKET BLOCKS

Make 12

Green Print #1 fabric:
Cut four $4^1/2$ x 42-inch strips. From these strips cut twelve $4^1/2$ x $8^1/2$-inch rectangles, and cut twelve $4^1/2$-inch squares.

Every quilt collection should have a basket quilt in it. The repetitive shape of the basket with the unpieced alternating block gives this quilt a clean, restful, and traditional appearance. The touch of appliqué adds charm to the quilt and interest to the border, yet is easy to do without adding extensive hours to the construction. The old-fashioned prints enhance this very traditional quilt.

FABRIC KEY

Blue Print	Green Print # 1	Red Floral	Blue Floral
Beige Print	Blue Plaid	Red Print	Green Print # 2

Blue Floral fabric:

Cut two 7 x 42-inch strips. From these strips cut nine 7-inch squares. Cut the squares diagonally into quarters forming 36 triangles. The triangles are larger than necessary and will be trimmed before the basket handle units are added.

Beige Print fabric:

Cut two $12^{7}/_{8}$ x 42-inch strips. From these strips cut six $12\,^{7}/_{8}$-inch squares. Cut the squares in half diagonally for a total of 12 triangles.

Blue Print fabric:

Note: Divide the Blue Print fabric into a $^{3}/_{4}$-yard length and a 1-yard length.

From the $^{3}/_{4}$-yard length:

Cut twelve 2 x 21-inch bias strips for the basket handles. The remaining 1-yard length will be cut in the Border section.

PIECING

Step 1

Position a Blue Floral triangle on the right-hand corner of a $4^{1}/_{2}$ x $8^{1}/_{2}$-inch Green #1

rectangle. Stitch together, and press.

MAKE 12

Step 2

Position a Blue Floral triangle on the right-hand corner of a $4^{1}/_{2}$-inch Green #1 square. Stitch together, and press.

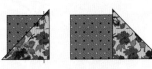

MAKE 12

Step 3

Sew the Step 1 and Step 2 units together. Add a Blue Floral triangle to this unit, and press.

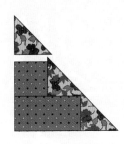

MAKE 12

Step 4

Trim away the excess fabric from the triangles, taking care to allow for a $^{1}/_{4}$-inch seam allowance beyond the corners of the Green squares and rectangles. Refer to Trimming Side and Corner Triangles on page 142 for complete instructions.

Step 5

Fold a 2 x 21-inch Blue bias strip in half lengthwise, wrong sides together, and press. To keep the raw edges aligned, stitch $^{1}/_{4}$-inch away from the raw edges. Fold the strip in half again so the raw edges are hidden by the first folded edge, and press.

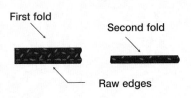

First fold

Second fold

Raw edges

Step 6

Referring to the Handle Placement Diagram position and pin the handle strip on a Beige triangle. With matching thread, hand applique the handle in place. Make 12.

Step 7

Sew the Step 6 handle unit to the Step 4 basket unit, and press.

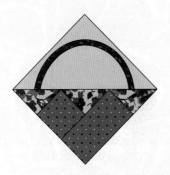

Draw light line using pattern.

Lay outside edge of handle on the line.

Use steam iron to help ease and shape handle to get rid of any fullness.

HALF OF HANDLE PLACEMENT DIAGRAM

Place folded edge of the paper on this center line for handle placement.

NINE-PATCH BLOCKS
Make 20

Red Floral fabric:

Cut ten $2\frac{1}{2}$ x 42-inch strips.

Cut three $4\frac{1}{2}$ x 42-inch strips.

Beige Print fabric:

Cut ten $2\frac{1}{2}$ x 42-inch strips

Cut five $4\frac{1}{2}$ x 42-inch strips. From these strips cut forty $4\frac{1}{2}$-inch squares.

Cut six more $4\frac{1}{2}$ x 42-inch strips to be used for the strip sets.

PIECING
Step 1
Sew the $2\frac{1}{2}$ x 42-inch Red Floral and Beige strips together in pairs and press. Make 10 strip sets. Cut the strip sets into segments.

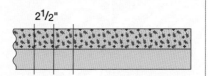

2½"

CROSSCUT 160

Step 2
Sew the Step 1 segments together in pairs, and press.

MAKE 80

Step 3
Sew Step 2 units to both sides of the $4\frac{1}{2}$-inch Beige squares, and press.

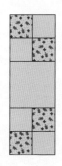

MAKE 40

Step 4
Sew $4\frac{1}{2}$ x 42-inch Beige strips to both sides of the $4\frac{1}{2}$ x 42-inch Red Floral strips, and press. Make three strip sets. Cut the strip sets into segments.

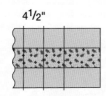

4½"

CROSSCUT 20

Step 5
Sew Step 3 units to both sides of the Step 4 units, and press.

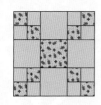

MAKE 20

QUILT CENTER

Beige Print fabric:

Cut two 19 x 42-inch strips. From these strips cut four 19-inch squares. Cut the squares diagonally into quarters to form 16 triangles. You will be using only 14 of these triangles for the side triangles.

Cut one 10 x 42-inch strip. From this strip cut two 10-inch squares. Cut the squares in half diagonally for a total of four corner triangles.

Note: The side and corner triangles are larger than necessary and will be trimmed before the border is added.

QUILT CENTER ASSEMBLY

Step 1

Referring to the quilt diagram, sew the basket blocks, the Nine-Patch blocks, and the side triangles together in diagonal rows. Press the seam allowances in alternating directions by rows so the seams will fit snugly together with less bulk.

Step 2

Pin the rows at the block intersections, and sew the rows together. Press the seam allowances in one direction.

Step 3

Sew the corner triangles to the quilt, and press.

Step 4

Trim away the excess fabric from the side and corner triangles, taking care to allow a 1/4-inch seam allowance beyond the corners of each block. Refer to Trimming the Side and Corner Triangles on page 142 for complete instructions.

BORDERS

Note: The yardage given allows for the two narrow borders and the middle border strips to be cut on the crosswise grain. Diagonally piece these strips as needed.

The yardage given allows for the plaid outer border to be cut on the lengthwise grain. Cutting the strips on the lengthwise grain will eliminate the need for piecing and matching the plaid outer border strips.

Blue Print fabric:

Cut seventeen 1 1/2 x 42-inch strips for the two narrow borders.

Cut one 7 1/2 x 42-inch strip. From this strip cut four 7 1/2-inch corner squares.

Green Print #1 fabric:

Cut nine 4 1/2 x 42-inch strips for the middle border.

Blue Plaid fabric cut lengthwise:

Two 7 1/2 x 84-inch strips for the top and bottom outer borders.

Two 7 1/2 x 101-inch strips for the side outer borders.

ATTACHING THE BORDERS

Step 1

Attach the 1 1/2-inch wide Blue Print border strips to the quilt, and press.

Step 2

Attach the 4 1/2-inch wide Green Print #1 border strips to the quilt, and press.

Step 3

Attach the 1 1/2-inch wide Blue Print border strips to the quilt, and press.

Step 4

Measure the quilt from left to right through the center. Cut the two 7 1/2 x 84-inch Blue Plaid border strips to this length. Sew these border strips to the top and bottom of the quilt, and press.

Step 5

Measure the quilt from top to bottom through the center, not including the borders just added. Add 1/2-inch seam allowances. Cut the two 7 1/2 x 101-inch Blue Plaid border strips to this length.

Add 7 1/2-inch Blue Print corner squares to each end of these strips, and press. Sew these border strips to the quilt, and press.

APPLIQUÉ THE SIDE TRIANGLES

Step 1

Make a template of the entire cherry unit to use for the placement of the individual shapes. To do so, photocopy the shape on page 135, glue the paper to a manila folder to stabilize it, and cut out the shape. Use the outer portion for the template, and throw the inner portion away.

Step 2

Center the cherry unit template on a Beige side triangle, aligning the bottom edge of the template with the edge of the Blue Print inner border. With the cherry unit template positioned on the side triangle, you can simply lay the appliqué pieces inside of this shape for placement to make sure all of your appliqué pieces are positioned correctly.

STEM APPLIQUÉ

Green Print #2 fabric:

Cut two 2 x 42-inch strips. From these strips cut fourteen 2 x 6-inch strips.

Step 1

Fold each 2 x 6-inch Green #2 strip in half lengthwise, wrong sides together, and press to keep the raw edges aligned. Stitch $1/4$-inch away from the raw edges. Fold the strip in half again so the raw edges are hidden by the first folded edge, and press.

First fold

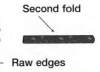
Second fold

Raw edges

Step 2

With the cherry unit template positioned on a side triangle, position and pin a stem strip in place. With matching thread, hand appliqué the stem in place. Repeat on the remaining 13 side triangles.

LEAF APPLIQUÉ-FREEZER-PAPER TECHNIQUE

With this method of hand appliqué, the freezer paper forms a base around which each leaf is shaped.

Step 1

Lay a piece of freezer paper, non-coated side up, over the leaf shape on page 135, and use a pencil to trace this shape 28 times. Cut out the leaves on your traced lines.

Step 2

With a dry iron on the wool setting, press the coated side of each freezer-paper leaf onto the wrong side of the green leaf fabric. Allow at least $1/2$-inch between each shape for seam allowances.

Step 3

Cut out each leaf a scant $1/4$-inch beyond the edge of the freezer paper pattern and finger press the seam allowance over the edge of the freezer paper.

Step 4

With the cherry unit template positioned on a side triangle, position and stitch two leaves along each stem with matching thread. When there is about ½-inch left to appliqué on each leaf, slide your needle into this opening and loosen the freezer paper. Gently remove it, and finish stitching each leaf in place. Repeat on the remaining 13 side triangles.

CHERRY APPLIQUÉ CARDBOARD TECHNIQUE

With this method of hand appliqué, the cardboard forms a base around which each cherry is shaped. This technique helps you to create smooth, round circles.

Step 1

Cut out a 1½-inch diameter circle or use the cherry shape on page 135.

Step 2

Position the cardboard template on the wrong side of the Red fabric, and trace 42 times. Cut a scant ¼-inch beyond the drawn line.

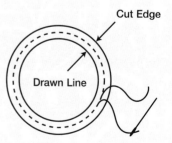

Cut Edge

Drawn Line

Step 3

Run gathering stitches halfway between the drawn line and the cut edge of the circle. The thread ends should be about 3-inches longer than needed.

Step 4

Position the cardboard template on the wrong side of the fabric circle, and pull up the gathering stitches. Once the thread is tight, space the gathering evenly, and press. Remove the cardboard template. Make forty two cherry appliqués.

Step 5

With the cherry unit template positioned on a side triangle, position and stitch three cherries along each stem with matching thread. Repeat on the remaining 13 side triangles.

PUTTING IT ALL TOGETHER

Step 1

Cut the 8¼-yard length of backing fabric in thirds crosswise to make three 2¾-yard lengths. Sew the lengths together along the long edges. Trim the backing fabric and

batting so they are 4-inches larger than the quilt top dimensions.

Step 2

Mark quilting designs on the quilt top. Layer the backing, batting, and quilt top, and quilt as desired. When quilting is complete, hand baste the three layers together a scant ¼-inch from the quilt top edge. Trim excess batting and backing even with the quilt top.

BINDING

From the binding fabric:
Cut eleven 2¾ x 42-inch strips.

Sew the binding to the quilt using a ⅜-inch seam allowance. This measurement will produce a ½-inch wide finished double binding.

BINDING AND DIAGONAL PIECING

See General Instructions on page 140.

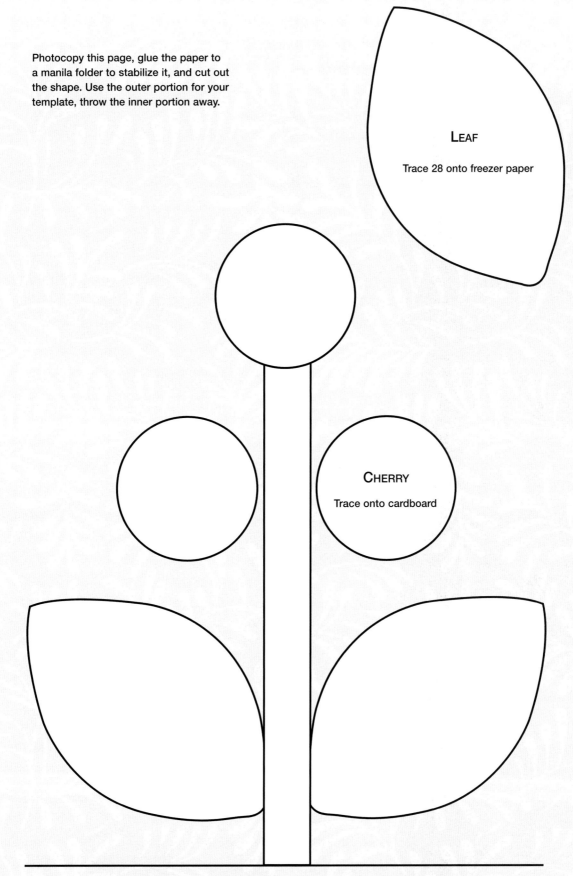

Photocopy this page, glue the paper to a manila folder to stabilize it, and cut out the shape. Use the outer portion for your template, throw the inner portion away.

LEAF

Trace 28 onto freezer paper

CHERRY

Trace onto cardboard

Align the bottom of the template edge with the edge of the Blue Print inner border

Flower Patch *Pillow*

Combining great floral prints and stripes makes a very decorative accessory, and the process couldn't be easier. Sometimes very easy, straightforward techniques and construction show off the fabric combinations best. Ticking stripes and florals are always a winning combination.

18-inch pillow without ruffle

FABRICS AND SUPPLIES
Yardage is based on 42-inch wide fabric.

- 8½-inch square of Large Floral for center square

- 1 yard Gold Print for pillow top and back

- ⅛ yard Dark Blue Print for lattice

- 1 yard Blue Ticking for ruffle

- ⅝ yard Muslin for backing pillow top

- Quilt batting, at least 20-inches square

- 18-inch square pillow form

- Rotary cutter, mat and wide clear-plastic ruler with ⅛-inch markings are necessary tools in attaining accuracy. A 6 x 24-inch ruler is recommended.

PILLOW TOP

Large Floral fabric:
Cut one 8½-inch square.

Gold Print fabric:
Cut four 4 x 8½-inch rectangles.

Cut four 4-inch squares.

Dark Blue Print fabric:
Cut two 2 x 18½-inch rectangles.

Cut two 2 x 8½-inch rectangles.

Cut four 2 x 4-inch rectangles.

PIECING
Step 1
Sew a 2 x 4-inch Dark Blue rectangle to both sides of a 4 x 8½-inch Gold rectangle. Sew 4-inch Gold squares to the ends of this unit, and press.

MAKE 2

FABRIC KEY

Large Floral   Gold Print   Dark Blue Print   Blue Ticking

Step 2

Sew a 2 x 8½-inch Dark Blue rectangle to both sides of the 8½-inch Large Floral square. Sew 4 x 8½-inch Gold rectangles to the ends of this unit, and press. Sew 2 x 18½-inch Dark Blue rectangles to the top and bottom of this unit and press.

MAKE 1

Step 3

Sew the Step 1 units to both sides of the Step 2 unit, and press.

PUTTING IT ALL TOGETHER

Step 1

Trim the muslin backing and batting so they are 2-inches larger than the pillow top dimensions.

Step 2

Layer the muslin backing, batting and pillow top. Baste the layers together and quilt as desired.

Step 3

When quilting is complete, trim the excess backing and batting even with the pillow top.

Note: To prepare the pillow top before attaching the ruffle, I suggest hand basting the edges of all three layers of the pillow top together. This will prevent the edge of the pillow top from rippling when you attach the ruffle.

PILLOW RUFFLE

Blue Ticking fabric:
Cut five 6½ x 42-inch strips.

ATTACHING THE RUFFLE

Step 1

Diagonal piece the strips together to make a continuous ruffle strip.

Step 2

Fold the strip in half lengthwise, wrong sides together, and press. Divide the ruffle strip into four equal segments, and mark the quarter points with safety pins.

Step 3

To gather the ruffle, position a heavy thread (or 2 strands of regular-weight sewing thread) ¼-inch in from the raw edges of the ruffle.

Note: You will need a length of thread at least two times the circumference of the pillow. Secure one end of the heavy thread by stitching across it. Then, zigzag over the heavy thread all the way around the ruffle, taking care not to sew through it.

Step 4

Pin the ruffle to the right side of the pillow, matching the quarter points of the ruffle to the corners of the pillow.

Step 5

Pull up the gathering stitches until the ruffle fits the pillow top, taking care to allow fullness in the ruffle at each corner. Sew the ruffle to the pillow top, using a scant $1/4$-inch seam allowance.

PILLOW BACK

Gold Print fabric:

Cut two $18^1/2$ x 22-inch pieces.

ASSEMBLING THE PILLOW BACK

Step 1

Fold the two pillow back pieces in half, with wrong sides together, to form two, 11 x $18^1/2$-inch double-thick back pieces. Overlap the two folded edges by about 4 inches, as shown in the diagram, and stitch across the folds, $1/4$-inch from the edge to secure them in place. The double thickness of each piece will make the pillow back more stable and give it a nice finishing touch.

Step 2

Layer the pillow back and the completed pillow top, with right sides facing. The ruffle will be turned toward the center of the pillow at this time. Pin the edges of the pillow top and back together, and stitch around the outside edge, using a $1/4$-inch seam allowance.

Step 3

Trim the pillow back and corner seam allowances, if needed. Turn the pillow right side out and fluff up the ruffle. Insert the pillow form through the back opening.

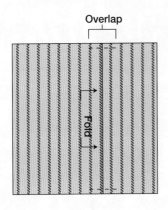

A **Welcoming Touch...**

Dress the bed with layers of different size quilts combining new and old quilts. Fold the quilts into different shapes and stack allowing different parts of the quilts to complement each other.

Use smaller quilts, such as lap throws or wall quilts, as accent pieces for the bed, draping them over the edge of the bed.

General Instructions

GETTING STARTED

Yardage is based on 42-inch wide fabric.

A rotary cutter, mat, and wide clear-plastic ruler with $1/8$-inch markings are needed tools in attaining accuracy.

A 6 x 24-inch ruler is recommended.

Read instructions thoroughly before beginning the project.

Prewash and press fabrics.

Place right sides of fabric pieces together and use $1/4$-inch seam allowances throughout, unless otherwise specified.

Seam allowances are included in the cutting sizes given. It is very important that accurate $1/4$-inch seam allowances are used. It is wise to stitch a sample $1/4$-inch seam allowance to check your machine's seam allowance accuracy.

Press seam allowances toward the darker fabric and/or in the direction that will create the least bulk.

ROTARY CUTTING

"Square off" the end of your fabric before measuring and cutting pieces. By this we mean, the cut edge of the fabric must be exactly perpendicular to the folded edge, which creates a 90° angle. Align the folded and selvage edges of the fabric with the lines on the cutting board, and place a ruled square on the fold. Place a 6 x 24-inch ruler against the side of the square to get a 90° angle. Hold the ruler in place, remove the square, and cut along the edge of the ruler. If you are left-handed, work from the other end of fabric.

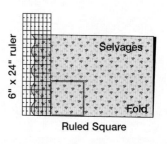

Ruled Square

When cutting strips or rectangles, cut on the crosswise grain. Strips can be cut into squares or smaller rectangles.

After cutting a few strips, if your strips are not straight, refold the fabric, align the folded and selvage edges with the lines on the cutting board, and "square off" the edge again and begin cutting.

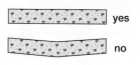

HINTS AND HELPS FOR PRESSING STRIP SETS

When sewing strips of fabric together for strip sets, it is important to press the seam allowances nice and flat, usually to the dark fabric. Be careful not to stretch as you press, causing a "rainbow effect." This will affect the accuracy and shape of the pieces cut from the strip set. I like to press on the wrong side first and with the strips perpendicular to the ironing board. Then I flip the piece over and press on the right side to prevent little pleats from forming at the seams. Laying the strip set lengthwise on the ironing board seems to encourage the rainbow effect, as shown.

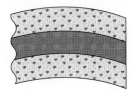

Avoid this rainbow effect

BORDERS

Note: Cut borders to the width called for. Always cut border strips a few inches longer than needed, just to be safe. Diagonally piece the border strips together as needed.

Step 1

With pins, mark the center points along all four sides of the quilt. For the top and bottom borders measure the quilt from left to right through the middle.

Step 2

Measure and mark the border lengths and center points on the strips cut for the borders before sewing them on.

Step 3

Pin the border strips to the quilt and stitch a $1/4$-inch seam. Press the seam allowances toward the borders. Trim off excess border lengths.

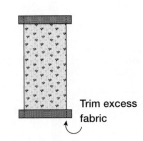

Trim excess fabric

Step 4

For the side borders, measure your quilt from top to bottom, including the borders just added, to determine the length of the side borders.

Step 5

Measure and mark the side border lengths as you did for the top and bottom borders.

Step 6

Pin and stitch the side border strips in place. Press and trim the border strips even with the borders just added.

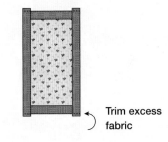

Trim excess fabric

Step 7

If your quilt has multiple borders, measure, mark, and sew additional borders to the quilt in the same manner.

BORDERS WITH CORNER SQUARES
Step 1

For the top and bottom borders, refer to Steps 1, 2, and 3 in Borders. Measure, mark, and sew the top and bottom borders to the quilt. Trim away the excess fabric.

Step 2

For the side borders, measure just the quilt top including seam allowances, but not the top and bottom borders. Cut the side borders to this length. Sew a corner square to each end of these border strips. Sew the borders to the quilt, and press.

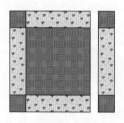

FINISHING THE QUILT

Step 1

Remove the selvages from the backing fabric. Sew the long edges together, and press. Trim the backing and batting so they are 4-inch larger than the quilt top.

Step 2

Mark the quilt top for quilting. Layer the backing, batting, and quilt top. Baste the three layers together and quilt.

Step 3

When quilting is complete, remove basting. Baste all three layers together a scant ¼-inch from edge. This hand basting keeps the layers from shifting and prevents puckers from forming when adding the binding. Trim excess batting and backing fabric even with the edge of the quilt top. Add the binding as shown.

TRIMMING SIDE AND CORNER TRIANGLES

Begin at a corner by lining up your ruler ¼-inch beyond the points of the corners of the blocks as shown. Draw a light line along the edge of the ruler. Repeat this procedure on all four sides of the quilt top, lightly marking cutting lines.

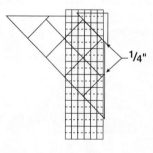

Mark cutting lines lightly ¼-inch beyond the points of the corners of the blocks.

Check all the corners before you do any cutting. Adjust the cutting lines as needed to ensure square corners.

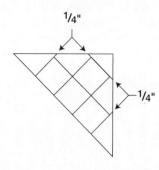

Make sure the corners are 90° angles before you cut.

When you are certain that everything is as square as it can be, position your ruler over the quilt top. Using your marked lines as guides, cut away the excess fabric with your rotary cutter, leaving a ¼-inch seam allowance beyond the block corners.

DIAGONAL PIECING

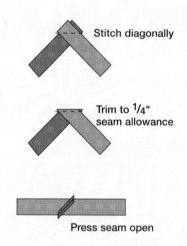

Stitch diagonally

Trim to ¼" seam allowance

Press seam open

BINDING

Step 1

Diagonally piece the binding strips. Fold the strip in half lengthwise, wrong sides together, and press.

Step 2

Unfold and trim one end at a 45° angle. Turn under the edge ¼-inch and press. Refold the strip.

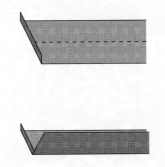

Step 3

With raw edges of the binding and quilt top even, stitch with a ⅜-inch seam allowance, unless otherwise specified, starting 2-inches from the angled end.

Step 4

Miter the binding at the corners. As you approach a corner of the quilt, stop sewing ¼- to 1-inch from the corner of the quilt. Use the same measurements as your seam allowance.

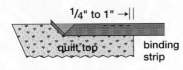

Step 5

Clip the threads and remove the quilt from under the presser foot.

Step 6

Flip the binding strip up and away from the quilt, then fold the binding down even with the raw edge of the quilt. Begin sewing at the upper edge. Miter all four corners in this manner.

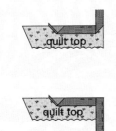

Step 7

Trim the end of the binding so it can be tucked inside of the beginning binding about ⅜-inch. Finish stitching the seam.

Step 8

Turn the folded edge of the binding over the raw edges and to the back of the quilt so that the stitching line does not show. Hand sew the binding in place, folding in the mitered corners as you stitch.

About the Author

Lynette Jensen published her first quilt pattern in 1988. There are now over 50 patterns in the Thimbleberries line, and Lynette is the author of 22 books about quiltmaking. Lynette designs the popular Thimbleberries fabric line, consisting of cotton calicos, flannels, and woven plaids, for RJR Fashion Fabrics. Her work is featured in major quilting publications and television shows. Lynette lives in Hutchinson, Minnesota.

Other Fine Books from C&T

An Amish Adventure: 2nd Edition, Roberta Horton

Appliqué 12 Easy Ways! : Charming Quilts, Giftable Projects & Timeless Techniques, Elly Sienkiewicz

Buttonhole Stitch Appliqué, Jean Wells

Curves in Motion: Quilt Designs & Techniques, Judy B. Dales

Free Stuff for Sewing Fanatics on the Internet, Judy Heim and Gloria Hansen

Free Stuff for Stitchers on the Internet, Judy Heim and Gloria Hansen

Mastering Quilt Marking: Marking Tools & Techniques, Choosing Stencils, Matching Borders & Corners, Pepper Cory

Piecing: Expanding the Basics, Ruth B. McDowell

Quilts for Fabric Lovers, Alex Anderson

Quilts from the Civil War: Nine Projects, Historical Notes, Diary Entries, Barbara Brackman

Quilts, Quilts, and More Quilts! Diana McClun and Laura Nownes

Through the Garden Gate: Quilters and Their Gardens, Jean and Valori Wells

For more information write for a free catalog:
C&T Publishing, Inc.
P.O. Box 1456
Lafayette, CA 94549
(800) 284-1114
http://www.ctpub.com
e-mail: ctinfo@ctpub.com

For quilting supplies:
Cotton Patch Mail Order
3405 Hall Lane, Dept. CTB
Lafayette, CA 94549
e-mail: cottonpa@aol.com
(800) 835-4418
(925) 283-7883

Index